Voyage to the Heart

The Nature of Love

Cameron Macdonald

FIRST COLOURCLOUD EDITION SEPTEMBER 2018

Part of the *Unified Love* series

Copyright © 2018 by Cameron Macdonald

All rights reserved.

ISBN: 978-0-473-45496-8

www.VoyageToTheHeart.com
Twitter: UnifiedLove

Cover Photograph by Volodymyr Goinyk/Shutterstock

To Denise and Amber
I love you both

Contents

	PREFACE	i
Part 1	THE NATURE OF LOVE	
1	What is Love?	2
2	Rational Love	8
3	Objective and Ideals of Love	12
4	The Three-Pillar Model	14
5	Journey's End	35
Part 2	ROMANTIC LOVE	
6	The Love of Lovers	38
7	Romanticism	39
8	Romantic – Being in Love	55
9	Romantic – Staying in Love	86
Part 3	ANIMATE LOVE	
10	Romantic Intimacy Not Included	91
11	Self Love	92
12	Family Love	103
13	Friend Love	124
14	Social Love	140
Part 4	INANIMATE LOVE	
15	Things Real and Imagined	147
16	Love of Things	148
17	Love of Perfection	158
Part 5	RELIGIOUS LOVE	
18	Love in Faith	173
19	Eros	174
20	Philia	181
21	Agapē	187
22	Nomos	190
	GLOSSARY AND TERMS	194
	NOTES & REFERENCES	199

Acknowledgments

For their support in bringing this book to reality, I have many people to thank. I am sure you all know who you are without my mentioning every name, but particular thanks to those who helped me through my first and very rough draft.

To Hamish Hesketh, Liz Kelleher, Richard Knotwell, Alison Starling, Dean Apps, Wendy Apps, Derek Quinn and Rebecca Webster, your help in working through challenging text has proven invaluable. Each of you brought another dimension of constructive criticism that has influenced the shape of the book. To you all, thank you. And Rebecca, for your inquisitiveness and encouragement, I am sincerely in your debt.

To Clare Wadsworth I am truly grateful. If not for your lateral thinking and precision in editing, the book would not shed light on love at all.

This book also owes its existence to innumerable discussions with my friend Justin Cook. We have covered many nuances of the work over the years. You often sent me back to the drawing board on key concepts — for which I thank you, although back then it was frustratingly difficult.

Finally, I owe a massive debt of gratitude to my wife Denise for supporting my journey. I say my journey: researching, writing and holding a career down was something I did, while you had our child, ran the household and managed your career as well as supporting me. I recognise your sacrifice and am truly grateful.

Preface

When I was four, Mum rang Dad and said "I'm leaving." She dropped the receiver into its cradle, stepped out the front door and left for good.

Over the years I wondered if she went because of me, if she ever loved me and if she still loved me. I have my own daughter now whom I love dearly. Amber is worth more than all the riches of the world. She is unique. Perfect. And she knows I will be there for her wherever and whenever she needs me.

When most parents tell their children they love them, that is exactly what they mean, without a second thought. But for me now I understand the essence of love, it all conveys so much more.

Writing this book has been a difficult but necessary journey, a voyage of discovery that started quite unexpectedly in a quiet, dusty bookshop on Manners Street many years ago.

There I came across *The Four Loves* by C. S. Lewis. At first, *The Lion, the Witch and the Wardrobe* leapt to mind. As a Briton, this, Enid Blyton's Famous Five and *The Beano* were a part of one's upbringing. The book's four rough white hearts within black-bordered boxes on its pink dust jacket told nothing more of its contents than its title. Worse still, its back cover carried nothing but publisher advertising. In fact, after picking up the skinny thing, it was clear its 140 pages were far too few for a fortnight in Fiji. Nevertheless, I read inside the dust jacket. "*With his characteristic insight, humour, and acute judgment, Lewis categorizes and describes all the natural loves.*"[1] That grabbed me! Does Lewis know what love is? I stood wondering, in a trance.

I took the book to Fiji.

Closing it, I placed it on the table next to me as I gazed across the still swimming pool. My wife, Denise, was chatting with her parents at the deserted pool bar. Fijian afternoons are so damn slow! I picked the slim book up again and read the inside jacket: "*Lewis categorizes and describes all the natural loves.*" What was promised and what I read were not the same.

Lewis' answer to love is deeply Christian. When he looks at love, he finds four types: Affection, Friendship, Eros and Charity. I cannot see how they apply to an abandoned child or the love of all wives by all husbands, or parents and daughters. In finer detail, he does not address differing types of love from self to things to ideas as I expected from a full theory of love. And, most striking of all, his book does not consider how people can say they love someone, but then act in ways that contradict such a statement. Or how love seems conditional and egoistic at times. Rather than describing love, it explains how to be affectionate, treat friends well, act in a romantic relationship and love charitably, all under God's gaze. This is neither love nor a categorisation of the natural loves.

What I need, I thought in that late Fijian afternoon, is a proper explanation of love: one that reduces it clearly to an essence that all types of love spring from, not a discourse based on religious belief.

I yanked the reins of my wondering mind. Lewis had disappointed, and there must be others like me who wonder what love is and have published their theories. After all, love is essential to life.

"We're going to freshen up for dinner," Denise called as she and her parents headed towards the hotel. "Will you be long?"

"I don't think so. Not long at all." That was 12 years ago.

On returning to New Zealand, I knew exactly what I was looking for. One book answering the question 'What is love?' covering all the natural loves, as promised by Lewis' publisher. I could find no such book, so here it is.

This book is in five parts. 'What is love?' is described in Part I as a universal or general theory. It is built on the 20th-century philosopher Irving Singer's theory of love. Love is fundamentally a bestowal of value upon the beloved, based on a sense of commitment and attachment beyond falling in love. By adding Plato's 'good', where the lover rationally seeks the good life with the good beloved, a three-pillar model of love emerges. This is presented diagrammatically as a single theory we can all relate to.

With the above in mind, the theory is unified in Parts II-V by characterising and describing all the natural loves.

Throughout the book I draw on well-known songs, films and literature to both answer the question of love and illustrate this answer. It is my firm belief that the ideas presented take on greater dimensions when you listen to, watch and, where practical, read about them. Love is contextual, and these examples offer rich context that reflects life. In the Notes and References, I give details for sourcing such pieces.

Of special note: although I have tried to avoid exposing plotlines in some of the references cited from popular media throughout the book, there are some instances where this was not possible. Regardless of this detail, as you read I would encourage you to pause and take the opportunity to listen to, watch or read the pieces mentioned before continuing. Should you not do so, I recommend you do it later with the work in mind to help consolidate your understanding of love.

I sincerely hope that in this book and in your own watching, listening and reading, and first-hand experiences of love, you will find what I was looking for.

Part 1
The Nature of Love

Love is a many-splendored thing.

Chapter 1

What is Love?

What I admire about history's great thinkers is their courage to question common beliefs within their fields of enquiry. Newton did when he wondered why objects fall to the ground, Galileo when he speculated — in the footsteps of Copernicus — does the Sun really circle the Earth? Newton might have been satisfied when he was told all heavy objects seek the centre of the Earth as God intends. Galileo could have been equally satisfied with the common knowledge of the Earth's rightful place at the centre of the Universe. That is how most people viewed gravity and the heavens in their day, but were these widely held assumptions satisfactory, they asked. We now know they were not, and their rejection of commonly held beliefs has advanced our knowledge significantly, benefiting us all in ways those men could never have imagined. This raises a question: what is common belief on love and does it match objective truth?

What Do We Believe Love to Be?
Listen to music, watch a TV show or movie, pick up a magazine or book, and nine times out of 10 you will find love. Particularly romantic love. We are obsessed with it. And not just as an idea but as a feeling. If we take popular media as a barometer of the human condition, everyone sees love as driven by an array of feelings, both good and bad, happy and sad, but central to life.

There are so many examples to draw from that dramatize the swathe of feelings associated with love. Most notable is Shakespeare's 1595 play *Romeo and Juliet*.[2] The elation felt by the young lovers and expressed through Shakespeare's vivid dialogue soon shifts to despair through the tragedy of their circumstances. These themes of lovers' emotional ups and downs have been repackaged and replayed everywhere over the centuries. And these days there is more consumption than ever of love's psychological difficulties with media on demand on Internet-connected phones, tablets and TV sets. In a contemporary sense, the 2001 movie *Moulin Rouge!* shows how ingrained the idea of feelings is when it comes to love.

Christian, an impoverished bohemian writer, is pursuing Satine, the star attraction of the famed cabaret club, Moulin Rouge. She is a courtesan seeking a wealthy man who will give her fame and fortune in return for sexual favours and marriage. In a critical sequence, Christian sings to her from the heart — through a clever combination of popular love songs strung together — trying to convince her to be his lover. She refuses, saying people should have had enough of silly love songs, referring to her rejection of love based on feelings. Love neither feeds nor houses you, she tells him. He disagrees and presses on with more sentiment from other songs, and she replies, again in song, that she cannot reciprocate his love based on feelings. She tells him lovers act like fools and throw their lives away for one happy day, predicting that should they ever become lovers he will be mean, and she will take to drink. She knows through bitter experience that the love he seeks is one of emotional turmoil. Arguing compellingly that love cannot be suppressed, he proclaims they should be lovers, and they embrace and kiss. As reflected in this sequence, and played out through the rest of the film, their loving relationship is a roller coaster of emotion from start to finish.[3]

Without doubt, the lion's share of Western media as reflected in *Moulin Rouge!* portrays love as an emotion. When it comes to romantic love it usually dramatizes the question many lovers struggle with: should I follow my heart or my head? Satine and Christian, alone and together, do the same as Romeo and Juliet. In both cases the heart wins out since most people believe love is a feeling or set of feelings.

It is not just arts old and new that tell us love is all about feelings. Philosophy, psychiatry and psychology echo the same message. For example, the philosopher Simon May, in his 2011 book *Love: A History*, defines love as "*a rapture we feel*". He expands this by saying:

> "*...we all need to feel at home in the world: to root our life in the here and now; to give our existence solidity and validity; to deepen the sensation of being; to enable us to experience the reality of our life as indestructible (even if we also accept that our life is temporary and will end in death).*"

May calls love, at its most basic, a feeling of ontological rootedness, which gives us the sense of home, solidity and validity.[4] These ideas resonate in popular culture. For instance Emeli Sandé on her album *Our Version of Events* sings to her beloved that in an uncertain and fragmenting world his love gives her a sense of belonging and comfort with certainty, where she can sleep in peace."[5]

Even though May does not say so directly, the ontological rootedness we feel "*at home*" with our beloved includes positive feelings of joy, trust, optimism, desire, passion, wonderment related to a happy life, as well as anger, frustration, jealousy, sadness and despair where love fails to run smoothly. So, his philosophical argument is clear: love at its most basic is not just a feeling proper, it is a set of feelings proper.

Along similar lines and more to the point, the late-20th-century philosopher Alain de Botton illustrates how love is all about feelings in his novel, *On Love*.[6] He explains in philosophical terms, how he met, fell in love, loved and fell out of love with Chloe. Both May and de Botton, in subscribing to love as feelings proper, have followed in the footsteps — and now remain in the camp — of many renowned thinkers and philosophers.

Psychiatry relays the same consistent message on feelings and love. Drs Lewis, Amini and Lannon in their book *A General Theory of Love* explain how the human 'limbic system' works. This includes several interconnected structures in the brain that between them handle emotions, motivations and behaviours.

We sense the inner world of our mind and the outer world of other minds emotionally. In relation to love, we use our limbic systems to connect with and attach ourselves in a loving way to those around us.

In explaining the limbic system as they do, Lewis and his co-writers believe love is a feeling they call 'limbic resonance' whereby, "*Two mammals become attuned to each other's inner states.*"[7] When in love, lovers become emotionally harmonious. We may see such unity through eye contact for example where there is a felt emotional response, whether between a mother and her child, two romantic lovers over a candlelit dinner, or a boy and his dog.

Beyond limbic resonance, or in spite of it, they emphasise two negative states of love: the first they call 'limbic protest' where the lover, when disconnected from the beloved, feels:

> "*…the inescapable inner restlessness, the powerful urge to contact the person ("just to talk"), mistaken glimpses of the lost figure everywhere (a seething combination of overly vigilant scanning and blind hope).*"

The second they call 'limbic despair' where…

> "*…Anyone who has grieved a death has known despair from inside: the leaden inertia of the body, the global indifference to everything but the loss, the aversion to food, the urge to closet oneself away, the inability to sleep, the relentless greyness of the world.*"[8]

We see these states when lovers are apart for extended periods. For example, in *Crazy for You* Adele tells of her restlessness — craziness her beloved calls it — where she wanders around the house alone muttering, opening doors and constantly thinking of her beloved. No matter how hard she tries to defeat her feelings and thoughts of aloneness, she cannot when all she wants is her beloved by her side[9]. The narrative of the whole song reflects Lewis, Amini and Lannon's view of love as a feeling.

Tallis, a clinical psychologist, explains in his book *Love Sick* how lovers end up in such emotional turmoil:

> *"There are many answers to the question 'What is love?' but 'A kind of illness' is one that appears (and reappears) with remarkable frequency."*[10]

He concludes that this illness brings about emotional turmoil of a profound nature that changes the way lovers think and the way they behave, where they:

> *"...feel less 'in control' and more volatile — less capable of making rational judgments."*[11]

With all these points in mind, current belief in many academic, medical and general circles is overwhelming that love is a feeling or group of feelings/emotions. Practising clinical psychologist Dorothy Tennon reported this in her 1979 book of research *Love and Limerence*. Lovers, she claims, display an attitude, sentiment, personality type, neurosis, passion, personal or religious experience, a mental state, a perverse mind-state, biological urge, weakness of will or obsessiveness. Beyond these descriptions, both from independent research and from her own, she concludes love, specifically romantic love, is essentially an emotional state, which she calls 'limerence'.[12]

But, just for a moment, forget feelings and states of mind and the West's obsession with them. If you listen to Rihanna's song *We All Want Love*, you will notice that in the chorus she makes three striking observations. All those looking to be loved want to be their lover's sole beloved; they want warmth in their lives; they want these things because the alternative is to end up alone and afraid.[13] These observations reveal something much deeper than feelings and states of mind.[1]

The first is a statement of possession. Exclusive possession. And when it comes to finding warmth, this is about seeking goodness. It is saying you want good in your life, not bad: shared and constant good with the person to whom you give yourself.

Finally, yearning to avoid loneliness and fear means you want somebody who is always there for you. Someone who is not only in attendance but also tending to your needs. But not just anybody. They must have chosen to be with you, and you must have chosen them. These elements together under the umbrella of being loved give you a sense of worth, a sense of value as a person in your own right.

Understanding what Rhianna seeks as a beloved through her song, you gain a sense of what a lover should be like. The lover must assure the beloved they will stay with them and care for them. They must choose to pursue a life of shared goodness and value the beloved so much that they always want to hold on to them. When you look at love like this, you see beyond the West's fixation on feelings and even the romantic.

---

[1] This plea by the beloved to be owned by the lover and to be warm and not fear being abandoned is a common thread across the West. For example, on her 2017 *25* album Adele asks a reluctant lover in *Water Under the Bridge* to be her 'keeper' and sings of how cold she feels in the wilderness — a wilderness where she is left alone without reciprocating love. If you look out for these themes you will find them both in lovers' and beloveds' messages.

Chapter 2

Rational Love

Rhianna's song *We All Want Love* alludes to a side of love seldom noticed, but which we know intuitively is there. The reason we fail to discern it is because popular media such as TV, film, song and literature portray the message of love as a feeling. The message has us push aside anything other than feelings when thinking of love, but we should sit up and take note. When the fireworks of falling in love are over and all you want in life is to be loved, what is it you really want? To be valued by the one who says they love you; to have them with you, caring for you; to know they are proud to call you theirs to the point of being zealously protective. And why? Because being together is a good experience, not just for you but for them.

The late-20th-century philosopher Irving Singer clarifies love when he defines the lover as *"...one who bestows value, and the beloved as one who receives it."*[14] / II

He goes on to say that the beloved becomes valuable as the lover grows attached and commits themself to their beloved. The lover does this, Singer says, through an 'appraising' relationship.

Reading Singer, I realised that, based on the lover's past, present and expected future interaction with the beloved, the lover bestows love upon the beloved out of choice.

II Although Singer in his trilogy defines value as bestowed by a man upon a woman, he does not limit it in this way. That is, the lover need not be male: she could be female. And nor need the beloved be female: he could be male. In fact, the beloved need not be human at all. The beloved could be any love object that the lover places value upon, becomes attached to and commits to.

For clarity, there are four points critical to understanding love:

1. Value is created in the beloved through appraisal
2. The lover bestows that value upon the beloved
3. The lover commits to the beloved
4. The lover becomes attached to the beloved.

So when a devoted husband says he loves his wife, he bestows value by becoming committed and attached to her. What he actually means is 'I value you greatly because I have a relationship with you; I assure you of my commitment to be with you and look after you wherever and whenever possible; I am passionately proud to call you mine.' THIS IS LOVE.

Appraisal
Before bestowal of love can take place, the lover must first appraise their potential beloved. In a romantic setting, we call this falling in love. Platonically, it is simply getting to know them. Singer relies on the romantic setting for his definitions:

> *"Even more important is the role of individual appraisal. The person we love is generally one who satisfies our needs and desires."*[15]

He goes on to explain that the beloved satisfies us consciously and unconsciously by way of ongoing evaluation through our constant interaction with them. The underlying point is that all loving relationships are appraising relationships. This is how the lover appraises the potential beloved and, where conditions are right, attachment and commitment bring about bestowal of value — love. Once love is bestowed, ongoing appraisal supports continuing bestowal.

Of note is the distinction between *"love bestowed upon the beloved"* and the *"perception the lover has of the beloved"*. This is extremely important as love bestowed is specific to the value, commitment and attachment which create and sustain the loving relationship. Perception is specific to how the lover feels about the beloved as the loving relationship is created and sustained.

Regarding perception, as a lover you constantly evaluate the present situation with your beloved while reflecting on the past and predicting the future. Looking back, you weigh up the good times and the bad, the highs and the lows, and conclude how you feel about your life now, the future, and your beloved overall. In conclusion, you gain a sense of what I call loving sentiment. In this context, loving sentiment is a view of your beloved within your own life, not based on one specific feeling, but a sense of your beloved's merit in your life overall. Where loving sentiment is high, you feel buoyed that your beloved is good in your life; where it is low you feel less so.

We hear this message reflected in the song (*I Love You*) *for Sentimental Reasons* sung by Nat King Cole. He says he thinks of his beloved every morning and dreams of her every night. His thoughts each morning reflect past experiences with his beloved; his dreams each night predict future experiences. Both, he concludes, are good overall.[16]

So, when he says he loves his beloved for sentimental reasons, he feels his beloved is good in his life because things have been good so far, and he expects them to continue to be good in the future. But, and here is the point, the reason for his bestowal of love is his loving sentiment after appraisal. This means he chooses to bestow his love, and his choice is based on reason.

Now it may be that he feels what many psychologists call love, and Dorothy Tennon calls limerence, and Lewis et al. call limbic resonance and what Tallis labels love sickness, but these feelings are not love on their own. They are part of the loving sentiment that informs his bestowal of love.

With these points in mind, Singer's theory is one of love rationally bestowed upon the beloved, based on the lover's perception. This is at odds with the conventional belief that love is an uncontrollable and irrational feeling.

Notably, Singer does not dismiss lovers' myriad of feelings, and neither do I. Love for most lovers is an emotional endeavour. But I am clear, even if Singer is not, that love is more head than heart.

In terms of love bestowed upon the beloved, when we think of love as a bestowal of value based on commitment and attachment as Singer suggests, we have the basis of a unified theory of love — one that can be applied to all types of love, not just the romantic. After all, we can value, commit and become attached to anyone or anything we choose where appraisal proves favourable. Furthermore, Singer's theory is universal as it applies to all lovers.

Yet, the theory as described in Singer's *The Nature of Love* is foundational. Singer offers nothing practical for the world we live in. If love is value, commitment and attachment as he says, what differentiates one type of love from another, and how do these elements apply to each love type? How do you love a romantic lover, brother, daughter, mother — or a photo, God, a memory or an ideology — if they all share the same foundation? Furthermore, Singer's theory is unclear why it is okay to love one person in a romantic sense and not another when we feel the same loving sentiment for both.

To answer these questions, we must build on his idea of value, commitment and attachment, beginning with the objective and ideals that lie at the heart of love.

Chapter 3

Objective and Ideals of Love

Love is the everlasting possession of '*the good*'.[17] This is what Plato claimed two and a half thousand years ago in his *Symposium*. The good he refers to is the idea that we always want things that are good for us — meaning things that gratify us in one way or another. Or, in reverse, we avoid things that harm us because we have a natural affinity for what does us good. The idea of seeking out good and holding on to it suggests that all we want in life is goodness and what supports this goodness.

Taken to its logical conclusion, we seek the highest good in love: a superior way of life. So superior in fact that the beloved sought by the lover is also good because he, she or it unlocks a way of life like no other. Therefore a beloved's absence brings about bad feelings in the absence of a good life — which the lonely lover seeks to remedy by finding a good beloved to spend a good life with. To this end, the objective of love is to *possess the good beloved who will secure the good life*.

This may sound selfish — egoistic maybe — in that lovers seek benefit from the beloved regardless of the beloved's welfare. But love, when rationalised, is not selfish. The highest good sought by the lover is one of mutual highest good, one where the lover is fully aware of the needs of the beloved and understands that to have their highest good the beloved must also have their own good.

This Platonic idea of love and goodness has been idealised over the centuries so that love's objective is the perfect beloved and the perfect shared life. Such modern idealism creates a loving relationship in your mind, and dictates what you must seek, and ultimately have in life.

In a romantic sense, the idea of the perfect life with the perfect beloved is an ideal we are all taught from an early age.

The Disney Corporation is a world leader in spreading this. *Cinderella*, *Beauty and the Beast*, *Rapunzel*, *Sleeping Beauty* and many more titles on Disney's list follow a well-trodden formula of perfect lovers coming together to lead perfect lives in a Western Christian way. This message is so familiar to us that we barely give it a second thought.

For example, the 2015 live-action movie *Cinderella* rattles off in formulaic fashion how romantic lovers seek and finally achieve the idealised good life. The wicked stepsisters and stepmother envy and oppress the perfect Ella. (Cinder)Ella's imagined perfect beloved and perfect life modelled on her father and mother's perfect existence before misfortune struck, the supernatural help in revealing her stifled perfection and getting her to the ball to meet her perfect beloved, the desperation of Kit, her perfect prince, to find his imagined perfect beloved after she leaves his arms so abruptly and the kiss that seals their romantic love create the ideal loving relationship of perfect lovers destined to live perfect lives within Christian marriage.[18]

Growing up into a loving sexual being, this ideal of perfect lovers leading perfect lives has been lodged in your mind. It is reinforced not only in childhood fairy tale fiction, but also in the general romantic fiction on TV and in the cinema, music and literature. The ideal is also given practical meaning in non-fiction editorials and glossy snippets in magazines, and through shared thoughts and experiences. The result is a well understood and accepted romantic love ideal spread across Western culture. And yet, never far below the surface is the normalised objective of love, both within romantic love and beyond it: the possession of the good beloved who secures the good life.

Chapter 4

The Three-Pillar Model

Value, commitment and attachment are the foundations of love, says Singer. We recognise such value through appraisal of the beloved. Taking into account Plato's ideas of love, at the core of appraisal lovers seek a good beloved with whom they will lead a good life. When idealised, this is a perfect life with a perfect beloved, but in understanding love this description goes only so far.

Love has a great deal more depth and breadth in knowing who your beloved is emotionally, and their knowing you, as well as the benefits of a loving relationship and the sacrifices made gaining those benefits. Love is also rational. You choose whom to bestow your love upon and whom you love — and commitment comes with that. Similarly, you choose whom not to bestow your love upon, even though in some cases you desperately want to. The same can be said for those who bestow their love upon you when they tell you they love you. And those who hold back such bestowal for their own reasons, even when they say they love you. After all, you are not free to bestow love, particularly romantic love, on everyone who may deserve it. So although the idea of loving out of choice is fundamental, we cannot set aside the emotional aspect of appraisal. For this reason, love must be considered on three levels with each one spanning Singer's theory of value, commitment and attachment. This diagram, The Three-pillar Model, shows love bestowed by a lover.

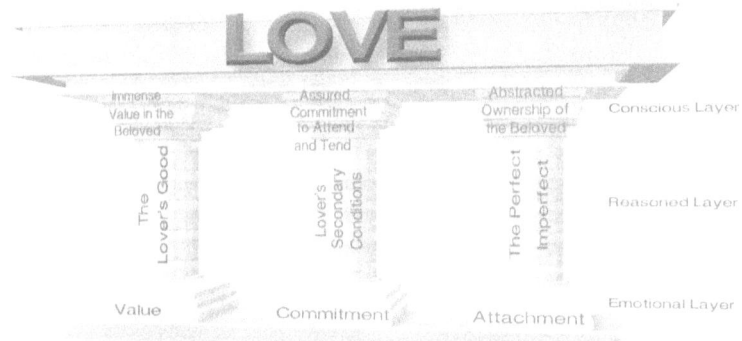

The Three-pillar Model

As you appraise a potential beloved, you build the three pillars of value, commitment and attachment, layer by layer, from the emotional layer up until you cap the pillars with Love by bestowing your love upon your beloved by telling yourself and them.

In practice, once you meet a potential beloved and as you fall in love with them, you experience rough and smooth times, and satisfaction and dissatisfaction. Through these experiences at the emotional layer you recognise value in the potential beloved as you become increasingly intimate and gain a sense of loving sentiment. You also offer a degree of commitment by meeting their needs and worrying about their welfare. In essence, you become concerned for them, and this is called 'robust concern[III]/[19]' which strengthens as you get to know them. As this happens to you, it happens to them during this falling in love stage. Finally, you become so emotionally attached that you miss them when they are absent and feel a sense of joy or wellbeing in their presence. Where there is reciprocation, you create the beginnings of what Singer calls an intimate society of two. The attachment, commitment and value generated at this early stage of a relationship are purely emotional. There is not yet enough depth and breadth for you to bestow love.

[III] Frankfurt, amongst other philosophers, contends robust concern is an ongoing desirous (volitional) concern for the beloved's welfare based on the lover's emotional relationship with the beloved.

At some point in the relationship, you will realise at the reasoned layer that the potential    beloved is the perfect person who brings the perfect life (in an idealised sense). This is because the beloved unlocks the good you seek, does what you expect them to do and has become your perfect-imperfect.

In recognition of these points, you bestow upon them immense value, confirm 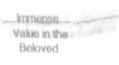   your commitment to attend and tend to them, and take up abstracted ownership at the conscious layer, which, assuming reciprocation, creates the society of two we are familiar with. You do these three things by telling them you love them and telling yourself the same. This final act of love's bestowal caps the three pillars, putting you into a state of love, which will stay in place as long as all three pillars remain secure.

This model and all the jargon are a lot to take in over a few short paragraphs, but these working examples cover each pillar and layer:

The Value Pillar

What is value? Most people would answer it has to do with money and what you get for it. The value of gold, for instance, is its daily price: how many dollars it sells for and how many dollars it costs. Its price can be compared to life's essentials and 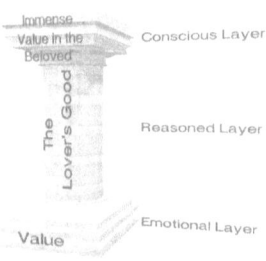 luxuries. A broader question is the value of a new car: Does it add to my social status? Does it look good and do I look good in it? Will it take me where I want to go? How much will it cost to run? What safety standards does it meet, and what does this mean in an accident? How reliable will it be? How does it drive? On paper, we can work out these benefits and costs and compare cars and ways of getting about.

Singer says these values are very different to the value lovers bestow upon their beloveds.[IV] He uses house valuations to explain, so I shall do the same:

Objective value considers several distinguishing attributes of the house. Aspect, number of bedrooms, location, access to amenities such as schools, shops, parks, transport links to the city, etc. Added together, these culminate in a monetary value reflecting an average buyer's future benefit should you put your house on the market. It is what someone should pay for the house without taking any feelings into account. Like gold values, objective value is a cold formula.

Buyer value is more specific to the needs and wishes of a particular buyer. The potential buyers value your house as if they might live in it. As you walk them around, they notice how well laid out the kitchen is and how the vast windows in the lounge fill the room with natural light. They tick their list of must haves: the large front yard and double garage, the open-plan living space that flows through to the outside where the family can sit in the summer months. These points and many others add value to the house above objective value. Objective value, where the valuer is aware of general attributes such as local amenities, the number of bedrooms and other house prices in the area, is not disregarded, but buyer value takes other qualities into account too. The difference is, buyer value is specific to that person in the same way car buyers buy a car for themselves, as opposed to a dealer who buys many cars for others. Buyer value, therefore, is not cold and formulaic, but not sentimental either. The buyers imagine living in a house without ever having done so, and this includes predicted emotional benefit without real past, present or future sentiment gained from living in the house.

Beloved value, in contrast, includes intimate interaction with

---

[IV] When I talk of lovers within 'appraisal' — in the 'falling in love' phase of their relationship colloquially known as dating — the couple have not bestowed love, meaning, not yet declared their love to each other. Where appropriate, 'potential beloved' is specific, but in a general sense in the 'falling in love' phase lovers have yet to bestow their love, whereas in the 'being in love' and 'staying in love' phases lovers have bestowed their love.

the beloved through appraisal. There are two distinct differences from the other two valuations in that:

1. It creates value in the beloved through an intimate relationship of emotional commitment and attachment.
2. Beloved value exceeds objective and buyer values as the lover realises firsthand the good achieved in the relationship.

Such a relationship includes loving sentiment past, present and future, and an appreciation of everything the beloved has done, is doing and may do.

Through appraisal, you discover your beloved is good for you, which makes them good in their own right. Together, a good beloved and a good life are what you seek in love. Thus the beloved takes on immense value by representing the perfect beloved who brings the perfect life.

Because of its nature, the lover's good as an aggregate of benefits cannot be determined. Nor should it be, as any and all benefits are purely subjective. Where love is present, should others determine how someone else should feel about it? That would be like saying sex is not sex unless one feels blissful in its execution. You can only ask the lover if there is a recognised sense of goodness where all benefits and disbenefits are taken into account at the reasoned layer of the value pillar. If the good is present the lover will say, yes. If not, no. So the beloved is of immense value where the lover recognises the presence of the good.

Although this idea of the good as a benefit has significant meaning for lovers and runs through common language and all literature and music, most people barely give it a thought. Ella Henderson, for example, weaves the idea of the good through her song *Hard Work*. Her relationship is not easy she explains, so at times she feels like giving up. And yet, despite the problems, she knows, in the long run her beloved is good for her. She recognises this even while she suffers emotional turmoil, and bestows immense value upon her beloved — to the point where she says her beloved is magnificent — because they have done, do and will do things that benefit her in tangible and, just as importantly, in sentimental terms.[20]

Bringing the good and beloved's value together to build the value pillar from the bottom up transforms emotional value into immense value at the point of love's bestowal.

The film *The Notebook* tells the story of Noah and Allie who fall in love as teenagers, but are pulled apart by social differences. Asking a reluctant Allie out on a first date, Noah appeals to her by promising to be anything she wants him to be.[21] This promise is important for he is offering to support whatever good she seeks. He wants her to value whatever she finds good in him and believes that he will find his good in a relationship with her — that good being the perfect life with the perfect beloved and the achievement of his own lover's ideal. So he needs to be a good lover who gives her the good she seeks. Soon after this scene, they pass through initial appraisal.[V]

From here, their relationship fluctuates as they fall in love — or appraise one another in Singer's terms — and the value they perceive in one another shifts from the bottom of the value pillar to the top in recognition of their good. The result: each will bestow immense value upon the other when they say I love you.

What *The Notebook* dramatizes up to love's bestowal and through to the end of the movie is a connection between all three layers of the value pillar. At the 'emotional layer', each lover interacts through appraisal as they fall in love, creating

---

[V] In the Western tradition, initial appraisal of romantic lovers usually begins through a random meeting of strangers, followed by increasingly intimate interaction. Initial appraisal is focused on aesthetics and early impressions with the underlying question of whether the potential beloved is the romantic perfect beloved. It ends when the lover believes the potential beloved meets the ideal, based on a limited exposure and when they consider themselves ready to be appraised by the beloved. The beginning may be their first encounter — perhaps as simple as a glance across a disco dance floor — and the end of initial appraisal is marked by the lovers taking on a sexually intimate posture as a dating couple. For some the beginning may be the recognition of a romantic attraction when a friend is suddenly perceived to be available, and the end may be marked by a kiss on the lips. There are no hard and fast rules. How long this takes is variable.

their own loving sentiment based on the past and present and a predicted future. In essence, one senses a good life of one kind, and the other of another kind, and together a shared life of good.

At some point, they recognise at the 'reasoned layer' how valuable their beloved is due to the good life they now share and which they were seeking from the outset: a life they hope will continue. This convergence of the good life with the good beloved creates belief in the presence of the good and they ask themselves whether to bestow immense value — love — upon the beloved at the 'conscious layer'.

However, bestowal of love cannot happen in isolation, as the remaining two pillars must first be complete.

The Commitment Pillar

When Singer writes about commitment, he points out that the lover adopts a posture that includes different activities undertaken with the beloved over the lifetime of their relationship.[22] Each activity reflects the lover's assured presence and objective as a positive influence in the beloved's life, while achieving the lover's good. In this way, commitment both 'attends' and 'tends' to the beloved.

To attend, the lover assures the beloved they will be a part of their life on love's bestowal. For many romantic couples in love this includes cohabitation, but not necessarily living in each other's pockets: one lover may seek independence more than interdependence. Another lover may seek dependence so much that they lose the sense of who they are without their beloved by their side. Therefore 'attend' does not mean to be with the beloved always. It means to be part of the beloved's life as agreed between the lovers, and may be high attendance as well as purposeful absence and, alas, times of absence in error. Attending as agreed between the lovers is important. It highlights the direct connection between the 'conscious layer' of assured commitment to attend and tend and the middle layer of the lover's secondary conditions that support this commitment.

As for tending, think how a loving captain tends to his beloved ship. At sea, he does what he thinks best for them both within a mutually beneficial relationship. We should never forget the lover's aim is to live the good life with the good beloved. With this in mind, tending has the lover adopt a posture as a whole. Although Singer lists a few things lovers may do when tending in a positive light — such as delighting in achievements, encouraging independence and developing shared pursuits — lovers also do things that, on the face of it, negatively affect the beloved and the relationship, at least in the short term. This does not prove an absence of love. It shows how the lover, within the posture of tend, seeks to bend the beloved and their relationship to their own will in pursuit of the overall good.

For instance, a ship's captain will sail hard through a storm knowing his beloved will take more than her fair share of its fury. He does this within the posture of tend as her lover. Do not consider this example an endorsement of physical or mental abuse, especially as regards this gender example. Tend is a posture applied within the goal of holding on to the good in the broader context of 'robust concern'. It includes both the welfare of the perfect beloved and the relationship, which may at times be at odds with one another. A loving father admonishes his wayward child by denying privileges, a jockey by pulling on the reins, and a romantic lover with hurtful words in a fit of jealousy. Although these acts go against the grain, they are part of tending within loving relationships that form an overall posture of assured commitment. Tend is not an idealised notion of goodness and light. It is a posture that pursues the welfare of the beloved for the lover's good when falling in love, and holds on to the good in a loving relationship.

Why does the beloved accept such rough and smooth from the lover? Because the beloved also seeks the good in falling in love, and ardently holds on to it when in love with the lover. However, this is not a measure-for-measure transactional relationship in tit-for-tat terms. There is complex interplay between the lovers when falling in love, and once in love. Each lover attends and tends in their own way when in pursuit and possession of their good against a cultural background of idealised selflessness. This kind of idealisation is discussed in Part II.

♥

When it comes to the mechanics of love, appraisal runs on two parallel tracks. The first is attending and tending to the potential beloved, and their attending and tending to you. The second is appraisal against secondary conditions up to the point of bestowal of love. Subconsciously you attend and tend to the potential beloved from the beginning of the relationship. This begins at the 'emotional layer' of the three-pillar model, where Singer's commitment means you just get on with being a dating couple — and beyond should the relationship develop into love.

However, regarding track two, both bring into the dating relationship rudimentary secondary conditions for basic needs, rights and values, and build on these conditions. The secondary conditions, as a kind of checklist, express the means of holding on to the good. As the appraisal progresses, the potential beloved will at some point fail to meet developing needs or to respect certain rights or share specific values. Aware of these failings, the lover must either force the beloved to change or accept the failures if an intimate relationship is to be maintained. Or reject the potential beloved. This awareness, imposing the lover's will upon the potential beloved and accommodating secondary conditions is appraisal at the 'reasoned layer', ending in whether the potential beloved achieves the secondary conditions by asking:

- ♥ Did they, do they and will they meet my needs, respect my rights and share my values?
- ♥ Where they fail, can I accommodate such failure?
- ♥ Did they, do they and will they achieve the good I seek?
- ♥ What is loving sentiment telling me in a positive versus negative sense as a condition in itself?
- ♥ Is this potential beloved the one and only — the

perfect-imperfect?

The answers to these questions are the basis of the decision to bestow love upon the potential beloved at the conscious layer.

This process is actioned in the 1978 movie *An Unmarried Woman*,[23] which tells the story of Erica, a recent divorcee who, after many years of marriage seeks a loving relationship based on freedom and independence having been denied both. She meets Saul who is also divorced. He is dedicated to his work as an artist and seeks a beloved who will fit into his lifestyle.

From the outset of their relationship, they do not appear to apply any specific secondary conditions to one another. They just get on with doing the things that dating lovers do. Within this context, their posture of attend and tend is one of emotional commitment unburdened by the pressures of their external lives: they enjoy each other's company, show robust concern for one another, and respect each other's needs, rights and values from an emotional distance.

Things change as they become emotionally closer. Saul tells her his work as an artist means everything to him, and how he sees his life with her, a life where Erica will have to compromise if she wants to be with him. His ideas of a shared life highlight several of his secondary conditions, which will be at odds with Erica's.

The transition from the lovers' 'emotional layer' to their 'reasoned layer' is distinct in this movie. In one sequence, Erica and Saul chat in a park about their life together as lovers — should they bestow love upon one another, and the secondary conditions that would come with such bestowal. This sequence clarifies what challenges many lovers: the lover sees a life where the beloved must compromise, and the beloved sees a life where the lover must compromise. The point of love's bestowal is when each lover must compromise — or not. At this point lovers seek reciprocated bestowal of love or reject their potential beloved.

During the closing sequence of *An Unmarried Woman*, Saul needs to know at the reasoned layer if Erica will meet his needs, respect his rights and match his values as a set of secondary conditions. Where she cannot do these things, he must accept her shortcomings if he is to complete his attachment pillar and assure his commitment to attend and tend to her at the conscious layer. The same is true for Erica. It becomes clear that Saul seeks a relationship of interdependence and constraints for Erica, while she seeks one of independence and freedom. Their bestowal of love is bound to these differing ideals. Can they compromise by saying he or she meets my needs, respects my rights and matches my values? And where not, can I live with these failures if it means my loving them and their loving me?

Not all dating couples struggle to agree on secondary conditions. For some, the transition from falling in love to being in love (regarding the construction of this pillar) is a smooth process whereas for others it takes time and many arguments.[VI] Where secondary conditions are fulfilled by a beloved meeting their lover's needs, respecting their rights and aligning to their values — and the lover accepting failures — the lover will construct their commitment pillar in readiness for love's bestowal once they have constructed the other two pillars, and offered the beloved assured commitment to attend and tend.

The Attachment Pillar

In his trilogy, Singer fails to explain attachment in any depth, except to say:

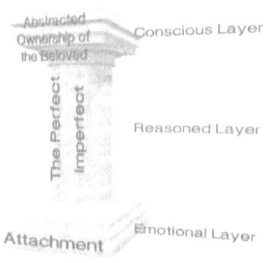

> [Love's] *"bestowal generates a new society by the sheer force of emotional attachment, a society that enables the lovers to discard many of the conventions that would ordinarily have separated them."*[24]

His message is clear. Through appraisal, lovers become

[VI] The three phases of 'falling in love', 'being in love' and 'staying in love' that you find in this book are drawn from Irving Singer's trilogy *The Nature of Love* and referenced in the Glossary and Terms section.

emotionally attached and, on love's bestowal, they are compelled to create a society of two. With this in mind, attachment should be viewed in two ways:

- ♥ As an emotion, or set of emotions, felt by the lover at the lower 'emotional layer' of the three-pillar model
- ♥ The society of two created between lovers on bestowal is a conscious one at the upper conscious layer.

Attachment in animals was first recognised in the mid-20th-century by Konrad Lorenz who observed geese and how goslings imprint on the guardian after hatching. Others who followed Lorenz' research include Harry Harlow, who experimented with young monkeys separated from their mothers, René Spitz, who observed orphaned babies when treated with low emotional involvement, and John Bowlby, who believed that mental health and behavioural problems could be attributed to early childhood.

This has culminated in the modern theory of 'emotional attachment': how we feel about those we care for and how much we want to share their life and have them share ours, although this does not mean love.

I believe this is what Singer refers to as emotional attachment, reflected in the emotional layer of the three-pillar model, and the group or class of feelings Lewis, Amini and Lannon sum up in *A General Theory of Love* (see Chapter 1).

Emotional attachment is not a feeling *per se*: it is as if absence brings about the realisation of attachment, in the same way you realise your dependence on a lens when it is withdrawn from your eye. Only when the world seems distorted do you understand how much you miss the lens, so that the joy and wellbeing of having it back strengthens your sense of well-being until the lens is taken for granted again. This is an oversimplification of attachment theory, but explains how lovers become subliminally emotionally attached during appraisal before creating Singer's 'society of two' when they are finally in love through love's bestowal.

And yet within their society of two, lovers want greater

certainty in holding on to their perfect beloved and their perfect life together, and so the lover takes 'ownership' of their beloved on love's bestowal, something Singer fails to account for in his definition of attachment. However the ownership I speak of is not oppressive — although there is often confusion by lovers and beloveds alike in this area of love. This is abstracted ownership in the lover's mind at the conscious layer, where the lover precedes their love object (noun) with the word 'my' (determiner) and seeks assurance from the beloved that their ownership is valid. This creates the attachment pillar: i.e. she is my wife or he is my lover. The lover calls the relationship rich in feelings at the emotional layer as Singer describes, perceives the beloved as perfect — or perfect-imperfect — at the reasoned layer, and as a possession within a community of two at the conscious layer. The attachment pillar is constructed from the bottom up in the same way as the other two pillars. The beloved accepts possession by the lover on love's bestowal as is clearly heard in Rihanna's song *We All Want Love*[25], and Adele's *Water Under the Bridge*[26], when she offers to be kept by her lover.

♥

At first, the idea of perfection may sound bizarre, but appraisal focuses on reconciling the beloved with the lover's ideal of perfection at the reasoned layer. We should not forget that the whole idea of appraisal is not only about knowing the beloved intimately, but about gaining a sense of the perfect from the beloved to assure the lover of the perfect life to come.

After all — and most lovers do not consciously realise it — the perfect life with the perfect beloved is what the lover wants most. To gain such a sense of perfection, you create a view of the beloved as perfect — or perfect-imperfect, because nobody can be perfect in an imperfect world. Once you create this view of your perfect-imperfect, you take up abstracted ownership so as to hold on to them as good, given they bring with them the good life. This is much easier than it sounds.

To appraise your perfect-imperfect beloved and take up abstracted ownership on bestowal, you first need a sense of their identity. This is not something new or unusual. You create an identity mosaic in your mind whenever you meet somebody for the first time, even if you have never considered identity creation in this way.

As you get to know a potential beloved, you collect 'descriptors': all the things they do and say in your company, and all the things you learn about them from other people. The significance and relevance of the descriptors result in clustering, and an importance rating for each that provides an identity mosaic in your mind of the potential beloved, which grows whenever you add or change a descriptor.

This mosaic reduces the potential beloved to many descriptors, clustered and rated by interrelationships, prominence and historical and future context. As illustrated above, some are more prominent (larger font) than others (smaller font) depending on their importance to you.

As you rate each new descriptor for relevance, interrelatedness and importance, and apply it to the growing mosaic of the potential beloved, precedence and importance change as they are matched to your love ideals. Achievement and failure — and acceptance of failure — of secondary conditions in terms of needs, rights and values are also applied to the beloved's developing mosaic.

While adding and changing descriptors, comparing the potential beloved to love ideals and shuffling through secondary conditions, you will be under the influence of falling in love. Your feelings will influence your perception of the beloved and potential as a couple together. In this emotional state, the mosaic of the potential beloved will take on emotional attributes embedded within your own identity mosaic, and the result will be a network of clustered connections between you both based on loving sentiment past, present and future. Now the potential beloved's identity integrates with your own as a sum of histories, thoughts and projected futures, giving you a sense of merger in terms of how life has been together, is together, and will be together as an emotionally attached society of two.

As the beloved's mosaic grows, the importance of emotionally positive descriptors tends to increase and emotionally negative ones decrease because of the wonderment felt during this falling-in-love phase of the relationship, bringing the potential beloved's identity closer to love ideals and creating a sense of a romanticised fairy-tale beloved and lifestyle. This results in a belief that the potential beloved is the perfect beloved, even though you are not stupid and know the potential beloved has flaws because everyone has flaws.

These flaws create a problem, however, especially as appraisal comes to an end and you need to either bestow your love upon the imperfect or move on in pursuit of your good with someone who is perfect. In *The Notebook,* Noah, narrating their earlier lives together during their falling in love (appraisal), says Allie rarely agreed with him.[27] She challenged and fought with him, and he cannot ignore these negative parts of their early life together without a remedy.

And there is a remedy: as potentially negative descriptors appear, you begin a process that includes two mechanisms, which together create a lovable identity of the perfect-imperfect beloved. The first is the 'Stradivarius effect', the second the 'veil of assent'. Lovers use these mechanisms iteratively during appraisal and reappraisal throughout their relationship, not in series as listed here.

To understand the Stradivarius effect, consider Stradivarius violins. As musical instruments handcrafted in the 17th and 18th centuries, they are highly valued and sought after not only for their rare antique value, but because some musicians consider their quality of sound perfect. I cannot comment on this, but Stradivarius violins are handmade from natural materials. They have unavoidable imperfections such as bumps, pits and planes of hard knots and softwood fibre. Their strings are not perfect and nor are the musicians who play these violins with bow ribbons made of imperfect horsehair.

Stradivarius notes analysed by an oscilloscope are not pure when compared with those produced by a computer synthesiser, where a sound engineer can remove all sounds not related to the notes to create what they consider perfect, pure tones.[VII] And yet, to the human ear, a well-played Stradivarius is richer, warmer, smoother and more realistic, and has many other human qualities when compared with the perfect, pure notes created by the computer.

The Stradivarius sound, therefore, when properly tuned and expertly played is 'perfect', in terms of the purity of each specific note played, and 'imperfect' with the myriad impure imperfections that surround each pure note. When such purity blends with imperfections the result for the listener is perfect-imperfection as both perfect-purity and impurity are combined. When appraising the beloved in a similar way, the lover welcomes the presence of imperfections along with the perfect. In practical terms there is something good about the beloved who always leaves the top off the toothpaste, shoes in the hallway and toast crumbs in the marmalade.

For lovers, however, when appraising the potential beloved and accepting imperfection, this is only half the story. All violinists play bum notes, and all violins fall out of tune from time to time. To anyone in pursuit of the perfect-imperfect sound, these failings make the violin's sound imperfect, regardless of the violin or violinist. Similarly, during the lover's appraisal, the potential beloved may do or say things outside the lover's tolerance, destroying the potential beloved's perfect-imperfection. Without a remedy, the lover will reject the imperfect beloved and take up the search for perfect-imperfect once more. To resolve this, lovers also apply the veil of assent.[28]

Imagine a translucent veil in front of your face that allows you to see through it. You may bring inside this veil any attribute of the potential beloved you wish to include in their identity mosaic, or leave outside any attribute you wish to withhold. In sorting out attributes, only those of importance to you regarding the identity you wish to preserve of your beloved may

---

[VII] Perfection and terms of purity have been brought together, suggesting they are one and the same. I say this to simplify the point. The underlying point is purity when stripped of subjectivity.

cross the veil.

If during appraisal you choose the toothpaste top, the shoes in the hallway and crumbs in the marmalade even though they drive you nuts, and add them to the mosaic, they become part of the perfect-imperfect using the Stradivarius effect.

During appraisal, however, you discover the potential beloved has a teenage criminal record for petty theft. Although you dislike the idea of a thief as this goes against a value you hold dear, you do not consider this descriptor relevant. For this reason, you leave the descriptor outside the veil to maintain the perfect-imperfect identity of the potential beloved.

Some descriptors may be so significant that you cannot deny them by leaving them outside the veil, although by bringing them in the perfect-imperfect you seek to maintain is at risk of becoming poisoned. You can do one of three things: 1) Include the descriptor within the mosaic and apply the Stradivarius effect, concluding that the potential beloved remains the perfect-imperfect by appending attributes and changing the descriptor to bring it into line. For instance: 'the potential beloved's staunch belief in rejecting abortion reflects their strength of character, regardless of such an unsympathetic opinion towards the women's rights I am passionate about. It is such strength of character I find loveable.' Here, you have decreased the importance of their pro-life descriptor and drowned it out with a character descriptor, which endears them more. 2) Change your own attitude to accommodate what would otherwise be their imperfection. For instance: 'the potential beloved's staunch belief in rejecting abortion is sympathetic towards the unborn child, whom I now realise has rights. The potential beloved's persuasive knowledge is something I find endearing.' 3) You come to realise your potential beloved is imperfect-imperfect with a high importance descriptor you find morally unacceptable. At this point, you will either accept them as imperfect in the short-term, settling for them as they are and leaving the descriptor as you try to change them into the perfect-imperfect you desperately seek during the remains of appraisal. Or, you will reject your potential beloved outright by refusing to bestow your love upon them and ending the dating relationship.

Once you create the perfect-imperfect in your mind through appraisal, there is a realisation that the beloved is 'the one'. This happens at the reasoned layer of the three-pillar model and means you are ready to take abstracted ownership of the beloved through your bestowal of love.

These appraisals are all about 'the one', the romantic beloved, but if the appraisal were of a friend or a car or a fellowship within a church group or oneself, then the role of the potential beloved during appraisal would be appended to their identity. You always appraise a specific role. This may seem unimportant, but it is not. For instance, love between romantic lovers, friends or siblings is very different and distinct, given that all interpersonal relationships have an aspect of role applied. Love always recognises that within identity when creating the perfect-imperfect, there will be an orientation of role regarding the perfect-imperfect lover, son, daughter, country, etc.

♥

Attachment has developed over the appraisal up to the bestowal of love whereby abstracted ownership of the beloved becomes necessary to hold on to the one and only for as long as they remain perfect-imperfect.

As far as abstracted ownership is concerned, no object, physical or otherwise, has embedded within it information as to its history, purpose or owner. All this information is in the mind, not the fabric of existence. An object may be a real thing such as a car, crayon, person or place, or imaginary such as a fairy, phantom, ideal or idea, or even a memory such as an experience, or a slice of time as a group of related memory objects, or a wishful thought.

For all love 'objects', you create and hold an abstract object in your mind. A discrete memory so to speak, which you tag with attributes such as purpose, history, relationship and relevance to other real or abstract objects, the reasons you remember them, and current and past ownership attributes. The result is an identity mosaic for each abstract object in your mind with the descriptors, in this case tags, clustered together.

The significance of tagging — and particularly the ownership tag you apply to abstract objects — is that the things you tag as owned are the abstract objects, not the real ones.

For example, I own my car, both in law and in my mind. It is a Lexus IS 350 and tagged with 1) registration plate — *[index]* 2) owned by — myself, my beloved car 3) bought by, and registered to, myself. This is the way most people consider things owned in law. But to tag the beloved as owned where you have no legal or moral title, you would have to hold an abstract image of the beloved to tag with 1) *[name]* 2) owned by — yourself: my romantic beloved on whom I have bestowed my love 3) free agent. You do not own the romantic beloved in any legal or moral sense, but you take up a posture of ownership as their lover upon bestowal of love, and in fact they want you to do this to show you love them.

There is no difference between your owning a cake, owning the experience of its taste in imaginative anticipation before you eat it, owning the experience as you eat it, and now, having eaten it, owning both the memory of the experience and the cake that no longer exists. It is this abstract ownership of objects that enables your ongoing benefit when you love them, regardless of their physical state. In relation to love, it means that the things you love do not need to have physical counterparts as a condition of loving them, and where an abstract object does have a physical counterpart, it need not be yours in any legal or moral sense.

The things people love may never have existed, such as a child's imaginary friend. They may no longer exist, such as a dead beloved, or exist as an experience such as driving a sports car with the top down, or an abstract ideal like nationhood or Catholicism. Or they may be real people and objects like a lover, son, daughter or hard-won trophy. This does not mean you do not love them. It means that you apply an ownership tag to the abstracted object just as you bestow love upon the real person or object. In doing so, the lover recognises the abstraction of ownership towards the real beloved.

♥

    As a working example, in the 1990 movie *Pretty Woman*, Edward is a successful businessman and Vivian a sex worker who both end up in appraisal — falling in love — in unexpected circumstances. They begin matching their romantic ideals to their identities using the veil of assent and Stradivarius effect. Edward must come to terms with Vivian's identity as a sex worker and her social standing, which he sees as lower than his own. Vivian must come to terms with Edward as a man who does not see her as his perfect-imperfect beloved, which she does by holding him at arm's length. Therefore he cannot assure her he will attend and tend to her in the way she dreams of being loved. She tells him her romantic childhood fantasy of being rescued from a tower by a rich, adoring knight on a white charger, but all he offers is the life of a demimondaine, available for sex and companionship at his convenience without the commitment pillar of love. She cannot love him on these terms.[29]

    As the film progresses, Edward continues to struggle to leave the descriptors that would bring Vivian's identity into perfect-imperfect outside the veil. When Vivian realises that he cannot love her as she is she leaves him.

    The hotel manager challenges him by saying that it must be hard to let beauty go.[30] The screenwriter, J.F. Lawton, brings into focus the lover's reasoned layer of the perfect-imperfect beloved (her beauty) and the lover's conscious layer of abstracted ownership (his letting go) to build the attachment pillar so that the lover wants to hold on to the beloved by taking up abstracted ownership. Edward does this by leaving parts (several descriptors) of Vivian's identity outside his veil and then applies the Stradivarius effect on what remains within, because the veil of assent used in this way makes her perfect-imperfect (beautiful). He also concludes the value and commitment pillars: Vivian is good as she will give him the good life and she meets his needs, respects his rights and matches his values. Where she fails, he accepts failure. He is now ready to bestow his love by taking up abstracted ownership of the woman he deems beautiful.

Edward's battle to resolve Vivian's perfect-imperfection is one many lovers fight. All lovers come to realise they must push certain descriptors of their beloved outside the veil if they are to reconcile the imperfection of reality with the perfection expected of love. In a sense, love becomes paradoxical during bestowal, and the veil is the means to solve this paradox and take up abstracted ownership of the beloved.

When Edward, Vivian's wealthy, adoring knight, goes to her apartment by limousine (on his charger), climbs the fire escape (up the tower that traps her) and rescues her (bestows his love) she resolves the same paradox. She builds her attachment pillar knowing he has remedied his perception of her through his veil and adores her as her ideal fantasy. Now she is assured of the good life with the good beloved in the same way he is, although he is far from perfect. When you watch this film, note the lovers' flaws. They have not changed who they are objectively, but the beloveds have changed their perception of each other.

When all three pillars are created from the bottom up, the capstone of love can be placed across the top. The lover achieves this by bestowing love and saying or thinking I love you. At that moment three specific things are communicated to the beloved and/or self. I bestow immense value upon you because in you I find the good based on our time together; I assure you of my commitment to attend and tend because you meet my needs, respect my rights and match my values; I take abstracted ownership of you within the role I perceive for you because you are my perfect-imperfect beloved. In this context, the lover bestows such love and continues to love out of choice.

Chapter 5

Journey's End

On my return from Fiji after reading Lewis' *The Four Loves,* I set out to find the answer to the question, what is love. I was sure that it had to pass certain tests: it should apply to all types of loving relationships and to all those who love.

Beyond these tests, it had to address two other underlying problems of love that I, and I think most people, struggle with: how can love be a feeling when feelings are transient, and how can love be bestowed one day and withdrawn the next regardless of any feelings?

The three-pillar model addresses the first two tests directly by showing love as value, commitment and attachment, which together are agnostic of relationship type and when applied top to bottom, emotionally and consciously, apply to everyone who loves. It is therefore a unified theory as it spans all love types, and is a universal or general theory as it applies to all those who love when they love.

Love as a feeling versus love as a bestowal means considering how we use the word in everyday language. When a wife says I love you to her husband, she is invariably saying more than just how she feels: she views him as immensely valuable and will be there for him wherever and whenever to do the kinds of things lovers do for their romantic beloveds, and she seeks to hold on to him zealously. Her words are active insomuch she is showing her ongoing commitment to him. In this sense the word love is a verb.

In contrast, someone might say they love in a less active way. Here the word love expresses their feelings: I love you means I feel like this when I am with you. Love in this context is not showing commitment; instead it is describing in the way an adjective does. The two meanings are distinctly different, yet

English is vague in getting this across. I call this vagueness the adjective/verb problem.

For example, in *Pretty Woman*, as Vivian lies next to Edward after sex, she says she loves him.[31] In saying this, she reflects how she feels there and then, not that she is committing to him in any way or that she likes him in the way a noun would reflect her comment. Really what she is saying is: I feel lovely right now, please don't make it stop.

The three-pillar model solves the feelings versus the bestowal test by supporting transient feelings across the emotional layer and assured commitment as a posture at the conscious layer. At this upper layer, the lover's commitment as a posture is held in place by the reasoned layer when the lover is satisfied the good remains, the beloved meets their needs, respects their rights and matches their values, and the beloved remains the lover's perfect-imperfect.

The three-pillar model is satisfactory in all tests, supporting love as a feeling where feelings wax and wane, as an ongoing commitment and being unified and universal. Therefore as a theory it describes the nature of love as a natural extension of Singer's *Nature of Love*.

Identifying love marks the end of a long journey — and yet is this really the end? My disappointment 12 years ago in Lewis' *Four Loves* was not solely that I disagreed with his explanation of love, but that the four loves he described fell short of my expectations. Affection, Friendship, Eros and Charity did not sufficiently reflect the loving relationships around me, nor explain how they operated. It is only by appreciating the relationships throughout one's life and how love affects and is affected by them that we ever truly understand its depth and breadth. Thus we leave one voyage of discovery and move on to the next: the categorization and description of all the natural loves.

Part 2

Romantic Love

*Clarity of mind means clarity of passion, too;
this is why a great and clear mind loves ardently and sees distinctly what it loves.*

—BLAISE PASCAL [32]

Chapter 6

The Love of Lovers

Romantic love is the love of a person, or thing, where the beloved is cast within a romantically intimate role. This love is unlike all other loves, where there are differing roles given by the lover to the beloved that exclude romantic intimacy.[VIII]

[VIII] Romantic lovers are romantically intimate in the same way as Allie and Noah in *The Notebook* or Jack and Ennis in *Brokeback Mountain* during their secretive relationship; Rose and Jack (*Titanic*) considered themselves intimate lovers. Romantic intimacy does not necessarily include the act of sex itself, but simply means the psychologically intimate posture taken up by lovers as seen in these movies before and after love's bestowal. The act of sex — if present at all — is just one small part of the greater whole of a romantically intimate romantic relationship.

Chapter 7

Romanticism

The backdrop of romantic love up to the mid-20th-century was Christian romanticism from a Western perspective, however, the considerable shift in social attitudes since the 1960s leads me to believe this backdrop has changed. We are in a new romantic era of liberal romanticism, which is very different.

It is hard to say precisely when the Christian romantic era began or ended. From the early 1800s there was an underlying cultural and moral view that romantic lovers should avoid doing particular things in public and alone. This was especially true in the falling in love phase of romantic love, but also, although not so explicit, in the being in love and staying in love phases. Lovers' sexual desires in both love or dating had to conform to cultural expectations and certain elements were expected from the roles of lover and beloved, such as he being the lover and she the beloved as well as idolization of the beloved by the lover, male heroes and vulnerable female damsels, spiritual fusion, safe harbour and everlasting love in the eyes of God — towards marriage, where sex was practiced in pursuit of children within the bond of marriage. All these elements have been part of the Western Christian ideal since the early19th century.

However, since the mid-20th-century several factors have brought about social change across the West: strengthened secular and liberal values, cultural acceptance of women's liberation, the acceptance and legalisation of same-sex relationships, the widespread practice of common-law relationships, and a general acceptance of sexual activity within relationships, regardless of the presence of love, marriage or the pursuit of children, coupled with the widespread availability of low-cost contraceptives. In these factors, the popular media's portrayal of sex and its place within the modern romantic relationship is most notable. This has altered the elements within romanticism to the idolization of the beloved (now equalized), male heroes and vulnerable female damsels (females less vulnerable), merging into one another (equalizing), safe harbour (mostly unchanged) and everlasting love (changing with secularism). Liberal romanticism rejects conservative Christian views of sex in pursuit of children within the bond of marriage and has also introduced sex and the pursuit of freedom into romanticism.

Without forgetting sex and the pursuit of freedom lie at the core of liberal romanticism, if we explore the five leading elements of romanticism: idolization, heroes and vulnerable damsels, merging or fusion, safe harbour and everlasting love, we can apply the unified theory to modern romantic love.

Sex and the pursuit of freedom

Popular media plays a significant role in telling us what we should and should not do. As an informer of social norms, it puts us under enormous pressure to engage in sex from the moment our romantic relationships begin. Not that people leap straight into the sack for the hell of it when entering a romantic relationship, although some do. This expectation of sex before love comes from a fallacy in contemporary media that sex is a necessary condition of love because lovers 'make love' through sex. This fallacy, now an integral part of the liberal romantic backdrop, informs lovers that to bestow their love upon one another sex must be a part of their relationship, and that sex before love's bestowal is not only culturally acceptable, but must be part of the relationship if it is to blossom and succeed. This is far from the truth.

In the 1997 movie *Titanic*, the liberal romantic backdrop portrayed by screenwriter James Cameron is inauthentic in terms of the era. In the early-20th-century, the act of sex between Jack and Rose would have been taboo.[33] Consider how an audience would react to the film in 1912. Rather than sex developing and cementing Jack and Rose's relationship — as intended by Cameron — an audience in a Christin romantic era would ostracise them and reject the film outright. Richard Wagner experienced such ostracism and rejection when his opera *Tristan and Isolde* was first performed in Munich in 1865.[34] The lovers and the opera were described as unholy and impure even though, unlike Jack and Rose, it was clear Tristan and Isolde loved one another because of a love potion.

The following is an extract from a widely-read English review of the opera published in London in 1882:

> *The passion is unholy in itself and its representation is impure, and for those reasons we rejoice in believing that such works will not become popular. If they did we are certain their tendency would be mischievous, and there is, therefore, some cause for congratulation in the fact that Wagner's music, in spite of all its wondrous skill and power, repels a greater number than it fascinates.*[35]

In contrast, a critical review of the 2006 Hollywood version of *Tristan and Isolde*[36] tells of a *handsome production* of *forbidden love*.[37]

These reviews of the same storyline are divided by just 125 years, and yet they are worlds apart. The former attacks Wagner's opera because of its 'unholy' passion (sexual content), while the latter cheers the movie's use of forbidden love but omits its unholy passionate content. In fact, early on in the 2006 film the couple's first sexual encounter shows their entry into love's appraisal, as most liberal romantic movies do.[38] Their continuing sexual encounters after Isolde's marriage to Lord Marke portray their love, so that in Christian romantic terms her relationship with Tristan is entirely sinful. Tristan's breaking the commandment of not coveting his neighbour's wife is significant in Christian doctrine, as is Isolde's adultery, yet liberal romanticism embraces such indiscretions in pursuit of romantic love.

Returning to *Titanic*, Rose breaks similar taboos and Jack has Christian beliefs to uphold in not coveting her as a betrothed, nor having sex with her, irrespective of the class system. The underlying question is, does Cameron choose the liberal romantic backdrop of a sex-centric relationship because the audience would not accept Jack and Rose could fall in love in any other way?

Cameron may feel that the Christian romantic backdrop is of the Old World — Europe before the mid-20th-century — and not relevant to passengers on their way to the New World of America, and that old-fashioned ideas of sex do not apply to Jack and Rose because Rose, as an American, has a liberal view of sexual freedom where women can put self before societal taboos and religious doctrine in the same way as men. One of the movie's themes is Rose seeking freedom: an underlying American theme in US nation-building. Whatever his reasons, for a modern audience to accept Jack and Rose's relationship as authentic it has to include sex, and that is what Cameron delivers.

To see the shift from the Christian romantic to liberal romanticism in finer detail, compare Shakespeare's *Romeo and Juliet*, and the 1996 movie of the same name.[39] Like Rose, Juliet is determined to be free to choose her beloved and this is what brings this play to life. The only reference to sex in the original play is Romeo's departure to Mantua after spending the night with her having consummated their marriage. This gives their relationship legitimacy, preventing its dissolution legally, religiously or morally. Sex has nothing to do with their status as lovers. In the 1996 Hollywood version of the play, however, the couple engage in sex in a scene that is not part of the original play as the screenwriters use sex as proof to a late-20th-century audience that the lovers' love is genuine.

Such modern adaptations of *Romeo and Juliet* and *Tristan and Isolde* — as well as Rose and Jack's story in *Titanic* — typify the liberal romantic message of our age. Love is developed, bestowed, proven and strengthened through sex. There are three reasons for this, which culminate in a modern view of the sex-centric liberal romantic relationship we practise today. The first is the watering down of religious influence, especially in the bedroom. In the past, sex between men and women was considered part of religious spirituality and morality. Sex was for procreation within the bond of marriage, not pleasure, nor to bring potential lovers together to cement their relationship. This conservative Christian view has been rejected since the 1960s as younger generations have embraced liberal values of self-expression and freedom both socially and sexually across Western Europe, North America and nations influenced by them.

The second factor of change is the widespread access to and use of low-cost birth control. The female contraceptive pill introduced in the 1960s coincided with rejection by baby-boomers of pre-Second World War conservative values and a message of 'free love' resonated through Western media. The HIV epidemic of the 1980s brought about a second wave of social change, highlighting the diversity of sex outside traditional relationships beyond the social change of the 1960s' free love era. It also clarified an acceptance of safe sex using condoms outside the traditionally safe sexual relationship, namely marriage. The culmination of these decades of change is the rejection of conservative Christian values. Men, and especially women, need no longer remain sexually chaste before marriage, nor duty-bound to follow previous social mores regarding sexual conduct.

The third factor of change is the release of women from legal and social male domination, empowering them to take control of their own lives and also to take what they want from romantic relationships, including sexual satisfaction, in the same way men have always done. Cameron dramatizes this in *Titanic* when Rose chooses Jack over her mother's choice of Cal and then enjoys sex with him. This to a modern audience underscores the freedom she pursues as her own good, which is the subtext of her romantic story in the film. The contemporary audience identifies with her pursuit of liberal and sexual freedom, despite what a 1912 audience would find impure and unholy, such as going against Christian duty, social conformity, chastity up to marriage and fidelity within it.

Titanic and *Tristan and Isolde* are two good examples that dramatize the liberal romantic backdrop of contemporary lovers against a Christian romantic backdrop. Both these movies show how central sex is to modern lovers, and give an underlying message of freedom.

Idolization

Idolization of beloveds by lovers is a carryover from 11th-century courtly love. Then male lovers idolised their female beloveds because of a perceived perfection that put them beyond reach. By idolizing in this way, their love could never be satisfied physically, but lovers and beloveds were satisfied spiritually through this distant adoration. The arrangement worked because the lover did not idolize his own wife, but somebody else's or a lady of the Court who was socially inaccessible to him. The lover married for property, procreation and sexual relief, so he did not hold his wife in such esteem or love her, although other men who rejected their own wives as he did might love her from afar. This social web of interrelationships satisfied courtly lovers' carnal and spiritual needs against a backdrop of Christian conservatism and courtly norms.

Today, such Christian conservatism, courtly norms, ownership of women as property and their use for procreation and sex has diminished, but idolatry remains a strong element of romanticism, although the emphasis has changed. In the 1993 movie *Sleepless in Seattle*, Sam idolizes his late wife when he describes her presence as magical and says everything was beautiful just because she was around. He makes it clear that when she was alive he adored her as a beloved who brought him the good.[40] His comment suggests he will only love another woman through idolatry as he did his wife. Annie Reed finds this endearing and pursues him. In Air Supply's song *I Adore You*, the lover asks his beloved if she minds if he adores her forever.[41] Both the movie and the song reflect the message of male idolatry where the inferior male idolizes the perfect female beyond reach, even when the beloved is accessible. Male idolization of women is under pressure.

Modern women now consider themselves equal to men and may idolize their beloved within liberal romanticism, as reflected in Miley Cyrus' song *Adore You*. She tells her male beloved she adores him; in fact, she says that she loves him more, in an idolatry sense, than he loves her, but at the same time, unlike courtly lovers and Christian romantic lovers up to the mid-20th-century, she, as a liberal romantic lover, seeks reciprocated love that is spiritually and physically equal.[42]

Miley Cyrus' song is problematic on two fronts: firstly lovers, regardless of gender, expect in a state of idolatry to perceive their beloved as perfect. This state must bridge the gap between self-acknowledged imperfection and their beloved's absolute perfection.

Secondly the beloved should reciprocate their love, knowing their lover is equally perfect in an idealized way.

Lovers who adopt the liberal romantic element of idolization overcome these two problems by creating complementary different and complementary perfect beloveds. The result is lovers who idolise one another equally on complementary but different terms. These different terms are most noticeable between heterosexual lovers, where the male usually takes on the masculine role and the female usually takes on the feminine role. The same is true of same-sex relationships through selective gender romantic roles.

The objective of love is to live a good life with the good beloved — and idealised this is to live a perfect life with the perfect beloved. In the West, the romanticized beloved female is the aesthetic, beautiful, vulnerable damsel, and the romanticized male lover is the aesthetic, handsome hero, even though beautiful and handsome are subjective terms. By defining the romanticized perfect in terms of damsels and heroes, the lovers mutually accept each other's perfection by fitting into the roles of 'perfect feminine' and 'perfect masculine'. The product is the 'perfect for each other' liberal romantic lovers who are often described as hand-in-glove, key-in-lock, jigsaw pieces slotting together, and even hotdog-in-bun. These complementary lovers are sometimes reduced to sexual innuendo, but they are a complementary different and complementary perfect element of liberal romanticism.

The song *L.O.V.E.* co-written and sung by Jessie J illustrates this complementary different and complementary perfect idea.[43] She thinks of her lover as a key, and of herself as a lock. By inference, when brought together she is unlocked and satisfied through their union. Her beloved's complementary perfection is that of a beloved who is good and will give her the good life she seeks. She confirms this saying they will keep her close, safe and happy. She thinks they seek to adopt a hero role within liberal romanticism, and sees this as satisfactory, although satisfaction is only achieved by their uniqueness as a key fitting a lock.

However, when it comes to love, exceptions are the rule. The notion of complementary different and complementary perfect idolized beloveds within liberal romanticism is foregone in times of mortal danger, when the hero will sacrifice himself for the vulnerable damsel — and the now higher value damsel will support such sacrifice.

Returning to the movie *Titanic*. We see modern equality in the hero and vulnerable damsel roles up to Rose and Jack's escape from the sinking ship. Cameron presents Rose as a young woman seeking and developing independence and equality as expected within the liberal romantic backdrop, but then there is Jack's sacrifice. There is an unspoken acceptance by Rose that she stays out the water on floating debris as Jack remains in the water.[44] Here both accept that the female is of higher value than the male. Although the movie dramatizes the Birkenhead Drill — where women and children are saved first from a sinking ship — it need not have been applied to Rose and Jack. But if Cameron had depicted Rose's sacrifice the film might not have won the Oscars. Unequal idolatry endures in times of mortal danger.

In a world where equality is closing the gap between the sexes, romantic idolatry of women where mortal danger is present will become doubtful. After all, if women believe themselves equal to men, they will refuse the sacrifice because male sacrifice stereotypes women as vulnerable damsels and devalues them by suggesting they are of higher value because they are more vulnerable. This infers that women can face dying less than men and are weaker than men, so valuable because of this weakness. In tomorrow's world Rose will not allow Jack's sacrifice unless she feels it comes from benevolence rather than chivalry or male romantic ideas of idolatry based on an old romantic stereotype. If the Jessie J and Miley Cyrus message is genuine, do they really love their beloveds more than their beloveds love them? Would they sacrifice their lives in frigid Atlantic waters for them?

Heroes and Damsels

In romantic terms, the ideal female beloved is an aesthetically beautiful vulnerable damsel and the male lover is an aesthetically handsome hero. Media bombards us daily with these images, creating the ideals they think we should pursue. Enrique Iglesias' song *Hero* gives a simple example of the aesthetically handsome male hero and the receptive vulnerable damsel, describing a man who will be there for his beloved and die for her should she accept him as her hero. He refers to this self-sacrifice in the last line of the chorus where he says his beloved can take his breath away. We see such an idea of a lover's last breath in *Titanic* when Jack perishes in the icy water, which we expect of him against the backdrop of romanticised love. Jack's act reinforces the romantic message that sacrifice by the male is a noble fate of romanticized heroes.[IX]

Ella Mae Bowen's iconic *Holding Out for a Hero* from the 2011 film *Footloose*[45] makes it clear that to a 21st-century audience a male hero is still a warrior, fighting and mostly winning against the odds, and returning bloodied and bruised to his vulnerable damsel.[46]

Most fairy tales give boys the returning or sacrificial hero gender role, which girls acknowledge, and define the vulnerable damsel gender role for girls who tend to their injured heroes, or lament their deaths, which boys accept. This is aimed at our children who, like us, begin their journey of romanticized love early on. The journey continues through novels, films, plays, operas and popular music that replay old myths and legends in ways they barely recognise, but are invariably more of the same.

Ovid's *Pyramus and Thisbē* is an example of early Greek tragedy where lovers seek the good in love.[47] It is reshaped by Shakespeare with *Romeo and Juliet* and by James Cameron in *Titanic*: the stereotypes of idealized lovers who struggle against a

---

[IX] This reference is gender specific based on the Enrique Iglesias' *Hero* video published on Youtube.com 2017.

world that denies their love, but it endures regardless and gives a message as potent now as it was to the early Greeks. Beyond the nucleus of enduring love, the lovers' roles revolve around handsome heroes and beautiful, vulnerable damsels. You are likely to seek what the popular media tells you about gender roles, presenting yourself in the way you believe others will seek you out within your own adopted gender role. If you are female, you will probably seek heroes, and in doing so accept the role of the vulnerable damsel. If you are male, you will probably seek vulnerable damsels, and in doing so accept the role of the hero.[x] Such roles are self-reinforcing. Everyone in search of love believes it is what lovers seek from them and the result, in a heterosexual sense — the strongest romantic influence across the West —, is that heroes and vulnerable damsels continue to be significant elements within romanticism, regardless of increasing sexual equality and changing attitudes towards sexuality.

Fusion

In Plato's *Symposium*, written in 385BC, Aristophanes speaks of merging lovers as soulmates. According to Greek myth, he says, we were one of three types of two-backed, four-legged, four-armed rotund creatures, with one head, four ears and two faces. These proto-humans differed in their configuration of genitalia. One had two male, the other two female and the third one male and one female. He tells the Symposium that in their arrogance they defied the gods, and to bring them down to earth so to speak Zeus had each type split in half and stitched up, resulting in the shapes and sexes we are today so that ever since our creation we have restlessly sought out our other half to become one once more.

Although such mythology is obscure now, the wish to rejoin

---

[x] Although this is not always the case — since the human condition includes numerous factors such as family upbringing, sexual proclivity, education and religious instruction — on aggregate, romantic gender roleplaying and perfection within it remain real and consistent attributes of modern romantic love based on supply and consumption of Western popular media as a guide of cultural desire and acceptance.

our kindred spirit has never left the human psyche and the message remains a part of the liberal romantic backdrop. You can hear it when Ricky Martin sings *I Am Made of You*. The second verse can be split into two distinct parts with the first four lines describing two lovers walking together through the adversity of life and the second four lines dramatizing their becoming one in the face of such adversity.[48] This conjures up two images: 1) a shared journey of two independent, passionate people heading to one calm destination 2) the fusion of two lovers who find calm within their shared destiny. The lyrics follow the process of love as the couple first fall in love through appraisal, then achieve the good they seek through fusion. Here, their good is uniting with their soulmate as in Aristophanes.

The next verse covers the idealized state of being in love through fusion as the inseparable lovers combine to lose their individual senses of identity.

The song is essentially about self-sacrifice and merging into a beloved's perfection, which is the same as saying you are perfect and my union with you will make me perfect, so we shall be perfect together after my sacrifice. It is at this point romantic fusion touches on other elements of romanticism such as the idolization of the beloved and heroic male sacrifice. This song also includes handsome male heroism and the beautiful damsel stereotype, since Martin is a handsome singer singing about the search for a beautiful woman with whom to merge and ultimately sacrifice himself for.

The imagery conjured up by the song's three subtexts raises a question of truth, as Martin cannot physically fuse with his beloved. Love begins in the imagination, defining the perfect beloved and the ideal life sure to follow. Once defined, lovers pursue the ideal beloved, bestowing love upon them and owning them. And this imaginative aspect of love inspires romantic fusion.

The second subtext is very much a modern spin on romanticism — the idea of fusion through sexual ecstasy. Since sex is a significant element of liberal romanticism, the idea of escaping reality through sexual ecstasy is both appealing and expected. In the past the sexual repression of women and the unspoken nature of their sexuality resulted in widespread ignorance. Sex was considered male release and female duty. Men did not merge with women sexually: they used them for sexual release and procreation. Now an open view of our sexual nature and general understanding of sexual intimacy encourages lovers to seek the euphoric experience of climax together.

The final subtext is the creation of something new. As outlined in the song, Martin sees fusion as self-sacrifice, where the perfect beloved will absorb the imperfect lover creating a new perfection when they come together. As the male lover, he considers himself inferior to his beloved. His sacrifice is the only way to join and be with his beloved in any meaningful way. Since courtly love denies lovers physical togetherness now and forever, the inferior lover, when he is with his beloved, spiritually now, or as a free spirit in the afterlife, must be consumed in that old version of romanticism.

But the male-dominated attitude of women absorbing their inferior lover in sacrifice is under pressure from liberal romanticism. Equal women do not want to absorb their lovers imaginatively or spiritually any more than they want to be absorbed themselves. Modern women would prefer to integrate as an experience where both lovers remain themselves. Such an experience transcends differences between men and women. Celine Dion's *Falling into You* extols this transcendental experience as she imagines falling into her lover and — assuming he is male — him falling into her. The result of this is not his sacrifice for her sake or his betterment, it is the lovers 'inside' one another, the experiential, temporary creation of something new where minds integrate and the lovers sacrifice their separateness in the moment, uniting into shared spirituality and becoming 'we' — separate, but a function of each other.[49]

In Dion's case there is the suggestion that sex brings about this integration where both lovers survive coming together,[XI] so she reflects a 21st-century sexual fusion on equal terms, a move

---

[XI] After she tells her beloved of her euphoric experience of falling into him, she asks him to close his eyes while she kisses him, after which she will miss him while he sleeps, suggesting she has been and still is in bed with him.

away from the older forms of romanticism celebrated by sacrifice.

Safe Harbour
Safe harbour addresses two fears many people share: abandonment and violence.

Most people think abandonment is being alone without a parent, friend or romantic lover to support them, but, abandonment in a Sartrean sense runs much deeper, where the universe is a hostile and detached place that does not care any more for us than an atom of hydrogen crushed deep within the sun. If you set aside other people and, for those who believe in God, God, you live and die without rhyme or reason, interacting daily with a world that cares nothing about your welfare. Secondly, you are free and the decisions you make are yours alone, even when they are made without understanding what their results may be. If you question your own basic morality and that of those around you, some decisions will cause pain due to unforeseen consequences as other people pursue their own good above yours, as you do above theirs. This detached and hostile universe, coupled with the predictable suffering from freedom to act causes the anxiety of abandonment.[XII]

The second prevalent fear is one of violence. Both fiction and fact portray violence affecting people just like you in wartime and peace.

Looking back at the elements of romanticism, there is an undercurrent that addresses the angst of abandonment and fear of violence in the adoption of hero and vulnerable damsel roles. The male hero role is an important attribute of the romantic backdrop as it offers the female beloved safe harbour. *Holding*

[XII] Although there being no God, nor original reason to be, and consequentially people are free to build up and tear down the very fabric of their existence is a somewhat Sartrean view, the fact remains, regardless of belief in the Christian God, that we live in a world of unpredictable consequences of almost all actions we take. For the non-believer the universe is full of ungoverned possibilities but for mathematic axiomatic laws. For the believer the universe is full of unknowable outcomes as God does what He wills with no one to answer to, least of all us. I believe we are free, and thus abandoned to an unpredictable existence and unknowable future while seeking law and morality to protect us from one another.

Out for a Hero defines this: the lover must win the fight against those who may harm his beloved. By doing so, and on his return, past enemies vanquished, he will protect her from all future dangers including the risks she takes in the decisions she makes.

Jessie J says something similar in *L.O.V.E.*, where her beloved acts as safe harbour, and most songs, movies and books with romantic overtones repeat a similar message that we tend to take for granted.

In *I am Made of you*, Ricky Martin says the lovers become one in the face of adversity. He and his beloved lead an idealized life, in peaceful calm, having absorbed him and his commitment to protect her. He uses the analogy of two rivers becoming one at their confluence; the ocean and these words conjure up a setting sun where two lovers, now together, are at peace in perfection.

Essentially, through their community of two, they create meaning between each other in terms of in togetherness, I am here for you and you are here for me, and our purpose in life is safe harbour through love. To this end, the beloved has overcome fear of violence and the angst of abandonment through his sacrifice in joining with her, although in the existential subtext he remains separate. That is because he will always rise and fight again to protect her because when all is said and done he is a handsome hero.

Everlasting Love

If love includes the good life with the good beloved, the last thing the lover will ever want is separation from the good beloved who offers such a life. In Plato's *Symposium*, Aristophanes tells of Hephaestus' question to the lovers:

> '*Do you desire to be wholly one; always day and night to be in one another's company? for if this is what you desire, I am ready to melt you into one and let you grow together, so that being two you shall become one, and while you live a common life as if you were a single man, and after your death in the world below still be one departed soul instead of two – I ask whether this is what you lovingly desire, and*

whether you are satisfied to attain this?[50]

Here, Hephaestus, the Greek god of blacksmiths and sculptors, asks the lovers two things: do you want to be melted together to become one? If so, do you want this in the afterlife? The latter question suggests everlasting togetherness, since the world below is the eternal afterlife to the Greeks. It reflects modern Christian belief, although the world below is equivalent to Heaven above, but fusion and everlasting love are not mutually inclusive as implied by Aristophanes. Love can be eternal without fusion and we see this distinction in the 1998 film *What Dreams May Come*. Chris and Annie are lovers who seek to overcome all obstacles and remain together forever. They are not as one, but independent loving soulmates who see themselves as such[51] and their romanticized love is close to, but not the same as, Aristophanes' story of the four-legged, two-headed, rotund creatures we once were. The film's premise is bound to Christian romanticism in that it relies on an everlasting afterlife of two separate souls being together and loving one another eternally. In this context, the lovers reject Hephaestus' proposal of being melted into one, and celebrate their everlasting love as independent soulmates in their community of two. This romantic message has survived the Christian romantic period and become part of liberal romanticism in the contemporary sense of Chris and Annie's independent sexual equality and everlasting love.

Nevertheless, the idea of everlasting love is under pressure throughout the secular West where an increasing number of people reject religious dualism (where the soul separates from the body and lives on after death). They do not see how, if you do not exist beyond life, you can love after death and there are innumerable examples where lovers commit to love their beloved all their life and stop there. Megan Trainor says just that in *Dear Future Husband* when she limits her love to her life span.[52]

And yet, contrary to expressing scepticism of dualism, everlasting love remains a strong message for many romantic lovers, because the imagination plays a huge role. With this in mind, many lovers continue to tell each other their love is everlasting, regardless of religious or spiritual belief.

The five elements of romanticism — and sex and the pursuit of freedom in liberal romanticism in particular — form the backdrop of modern romantic love although not all lovers embrace all elements. Some may reject out of hand the idea of merging and others may consider heroes and vulnerable damsels trite and reject such a notion. Nevertheless, romanticism, particularly liberal romanticism, remains as a cultural backdrop of the modern relationship for the foreseeable future, made inevitable by the presence and strength of media and cultural influence on the contemporary couple.

Chapter 8

Romantic – Being in Love

I love you. I love you too. These words mark the beginning of being in love for romantic lovers — a true state of being when the three pillars are in place for both lovers and capped with Love. As well as such bestowal there are basic secondary conditions, which each lover will seek to build on during their relationship, although this process will be challenged as compromises must be made by the lovers as their relationship deepens and broadens. They will continue to pursue their good, while holding on to their sense of the perfect-imperfect beloved.

Some secondary conditions associated with romantic love, such as fidelity, selflessness, honesty and trust, contradict innate human traits such as infidelity, selfishness, lies and jealousy, and are extremely difficult to live up to.

For instance, selfishness and selflessness are at opposite ends of a continuum we all experience in life. Lovers seek selflessness from each other, but are also selfish in the good they pursue. The same is true of jealousy and trust. Below the surface, lovers who cannot help but feel anxious that their beloved will be lured away by another potential lover demand unwavering trust. Since jealousy is such a primal emotion, as Othello discovers in Shakespeare's play of the same name, it is hard for lovers to trust their beloved completely, especially in this phase of love.

As many secondary conditions contradict one another, they risk each lover's good, and the identity of the perfect-imperfect beloved too. For this reason, especially in the early years, the state of being in love tends to include many points of reappraisal, where lovers take stock of their expectations regarding needs, rights and values, loving sentiment and their ongoing perception of their perfect-imperfect beloved. All of this takes time, and so this phase of being in love lasts for many years and is at times like riding a roller coaster — one that begins with high optimism on love's bestowal, followed by travelling up and down to a destination of either contented, relative calm or disappointed rejection. In the former, the loving relationship moves to its final phase of staying in love, in the latter to separation.

Fallin', sung by Alicia Keys, illustrates the up and down nature of being in love and her struggles to come to terms with the ongoing challenges in her loving relationship, which force her into reappraisal. One challenge is a sense of exploitation and feeling this secondary condition is failing and she must confront her beloved or, worse, reject them altogether by withdrawing her love.[53]

As lovers struggle with secondary conditions, they also struggle to maintain their perception of the perfect-imperfect beloved, especially within the context of the life they share. When falling in love, lovers use the Stradivarius effect and veil of assent under the influence of rose-tinted glasses but, once emotional bonding is over and the rose-tint gone, they perceive their beloveds differently and, as here, with less tolerance. When falling in love, Alicia's potential beloved's identity does not include selfishness, but now she may have to add this descriptor as it becomes evident and she seeks a remedy.

For most loving couples, achieving their good, building on and working through secondary conditions and maintaining their beloved's perfect-imperfect identity is not insurmountable. Where successful, lovers, as a community of two, move on to staying in love, usually the zenith of their romantic loving relationship.

Achieving the Lover's Good

Most romantic lovers consider their relationship safe harbour from a hostile world, and in many cases battling this hostile world together strengthens the bond between them. For instance, Romeo and Juliet's warring families bring about anguish which reinforces their relationship in the same way comrade love is braced through shared conflict against a common enemy. Had Romeo and Juliet survived their tragedy, they could never have escaped the hostility of their warring families who would have continued to try to destroy their relationship. Juliet's father was clear: if you reject Paris' hand in marriage you will, '*hang, beg, starve, die in the streets.*'[54] Through his rejection of her — and Romeo's family's rejection of him once he had married a Capulet — the couple would have struggled against a hostile world. And yet, this struggle might have united them more as it does most couples. By fighting in unity, they survive in unity because love conquers all. This is a message that bonds lovers instead of breaking them.

Yet, contradictory as it may sound, conflict between lovers unites them too, bringing about, in a strange twist, conflict that many lovers seek. This comes through feelings of misunderstanding as to each other's place in the world, abandonment, anger, and even frustrated hatred when one fails to bend to the other's will. This uniting internal conflict raises the question of why romantic lovers find benefit in conflict when another benefit they seek is harmony in peaceful perfection — after all, love is a 'live happily ever after' ideal with the perfect beloved dramatized in fairy tales. Such fairy-tale endings never depict conflict within the community of two. The answer is existential conflict. Every human being carries psychological issues that create existential conflict and, through love, seek its remedy, which is a part of the lover's good in itself.

Existential Conflict
The 20th-century philosopher and Nobel laureate, Jean-Paul Sartre reduced the human condition to the following feelings:

1. We are in a constant struggle to understand who we are
2. We are in a state of existential angst because we feel anguish, abandonment and despair in that:
   a. We know our decisions change the lives of those around us
   b. We know we are alone in a world indifferent towards us

c. We act in the hope of outcomes in a world of possibilities.[55]

Regarding the struggle to understand who we are: you cannot see your psychological self directly because you cannot step outside your mind to look back at yourself. The only way you can see yourself and figure out who you are psychologically is through the reflection of others, and seeing yourself through the reflection of your beloved is one of the benefits love brings.

Lovers are often challenged by the difference between whom they believe themselves to be and the identity reflected by their beloved — and the mismatch between these two identities introduces conflict. The degree of conflict depends on the emotional closeness between lovers and the ideals each has of their perfect-imperfect beloved and life ahead.

Trust, equality and selflessness play significant roles in emotional closeness. If your relationship includes all three — as seen in friendship — differences in your view of your identity and that reflected to you by your beloved will be minor, and yet there is a subtle dynamic going on here. Honest reflections at odds with the beloved's ideal are remedied by the lover to meet the beloved's ideal.

This means that, by loving you, your beloved both shapes and reflects your identity more closely to who you are and whom they want you to be; in turn, you shape yourself closer to what you believe your beloved wants you to be and who you want to be. The result is a complementary loop of what they want and who you are, which come together to create an actual shared love ideal. In practice, this is achieved by your beloved — as your lover — bringing into their veil of assent attributes that others would reject as you in turn change your behaviour to lower the importance and suppress negative attributes. The result is you — your identity as reflected by your beloved — their perfect-imperfect, once smoothed by their Stradivarius effect.

In loving relationships where a complementary loop exists, conflict tends to be low as each lover embraces their reflection from their beloved in full, given the perfect-imperfect is always reflected back as each lover strives to maintain this identity.

This low conflict relationship is seen in the 1990 French movie *Le mari de la coiffeuse* (*The Hairdresser's Husband*). In his mind, Antoine creates an idealized romantic beloved based on a hairdresser he visited at the age of 12. Later in life he meets Mathilde, his real ideal beloved, another hairdresser who loves him in return and in a pivotal scene as they dance, Antoine holds her tight. Mathilde is fearful he may one day reject her as she ages, but Antoine says he will always want to hold her like this and assures her he asks nothing of her. As her lover, he seeks no change from her identity now or in the future. To him, she is and will always be his perfect-imperfect, and this is what he reflects to her.[56]

As this film is about Antoine's unchanging idealization of romantic love, it highlights that Mathilde is in body and mind (identity) what he wants her to be: beautiful and unchanging. Conflict is low in their relationship because he reflects her perfect-imperfection as he sees it and she, up to this point, has accepted this reflection and worked to maintain it.

Yet she fears her identity's fragility because such a reflection is not in reality as timeless as he suggests, especially aesthetically. Her looks are an attribute of her identity beyond her control, and she knows that they will deteriorate even though idealism rejects this. This is a point of conflict as one of the benefits she seeks in romantic love is a deep understanding of self from Antoine, which she achieves in an idealized sense. This understanding has come from the trust, equality and selflessness which has been the mainstay of their relationship, but for Mathilde there is a tipping point which the film dramatizes.

In relationships where these three attributes are scarce, there is a mismatch between the identity reflected and your view of yourself, so that if in this context you seek an understanding of self as a benefit towards your good in love, there will be conflict. This is especially true where your beloved seeks to mould you to their love ideal to achieve their own good in loving you — their perfect beloved with whom they will lead their perfect life. In such a relationship, you will be under pressure to change to their ideal beloved's identity and, as pressure mounts, you will resist changing what you do and say because you resent their inability to accept you for what you believe yourself to be. Your resistance to change introduces distrust in your reflection from them because they taint your identity by their ideas of your imperfections.

This is the basis of Christina Perri's song *Human,* in which she pleads with her beloved to relieve her of the perfection they seek in loving her. What is striking about her song is how relationships play out in reality when the beloved as a lover idealizes their lover, in this case Christina, who seeks an understanding of self. At first she accepts their reflection of self as imperfect, because understanding self is a benefit sought in love, but on acceptance of the imperfect she tries to become her lover's ideal (perfect). When she realises she cannot achieve this, disbelief in her lover's reflection of her identity brings on conflict, which she understands as lack of trust, equality and a sense of selfishness in her lover.[57]

Therefore romantic relationships with lower levels of trust, equality and selflessness become problematic as they hamper one of the benefits sought by the lover: a true sense of self. As this happens, lovers appeal to their beloveds to stop trying to make them into their version of perfect and it is at this point that conflict arises. This is what *Human* is about: accept me for who I believe myself to be and, as my lover, reflect to me that I am your perfect-imperfect because I need to know I am who I think I am, not the imperfect you say I am. In failing this, I will break down like any other human being. And beware, there will come a point when I will take no more and withdraw my love from you.

Unfortunately, our effort in getting to know self intimately is often a flashpoint within the being in love phase, because getting to know oneself can be a humbling experience that breaks some lovers apart — but one that can unite others through the experience of discovery. After all, lovers want to be each other's perfect-imperfect and live a shared good life and do so through gaining a deep and broad understanding of one another within their intimate society of two.

♥

In several of his works, Sartre shows how human it is to feel anguish, abandonment and despair.[58] Irvin Yalom, a respected 20th-century clinical psychologist, develops Sartre's ideas further in his 1989 book *Love's Executioner and Other Tales of Psychology*. He coins the term 'existence pain' which includes four givens that lie beneath our thoughts and actions:

1. The inevitability of death for us and those we love
2. The freedom to make our lives as we will
3. Our ultimate aloneness
4. An absence of any obvious meaning or sense to life.[59]

Yalom's four givens roughly match Simon May's idea of ontological rootedness: ...*[3]we all need to feel at home in the world: to root our life in the here and now; to [4]give our existence solidity and validity; to [2]deepen the sensation of being; to [1]enable us to experience the reality of our life as indestructible (even if we also accept that our life is temporary and will end in death).*[60]

When we consider Sartre, Yalom and May's ideas together, it becomes clear where potential conflict lies. If nobody loves you — if there is a total absence of love, including God's love — the world is a lonely place and, death looks like a lonely looming affair, so you wonder if anything in this world will bend to your will. These points feel especially true where you seek love against constant rejection. If somebody does love you but they disregard your existence pain, such feelings and questions surface and anything they may have done to set your mind at ease, and you theirs, will be eroded and eventually lost.

In Atom Egoyan's 1994 film *Exotica*, Francis' daughter and wife are dead and in his car one evening he asks his niece, Tracey, who still comes to his house to babysit his daughter who no longer exists, if she ever feels she did not ask to be brought into the world. She does. He now wonders, who is asking him to stay.[61]

Francis has outlived his wife and daughter, and the good life they once shared, a life where there was the good of May's ontological rootedness, and Yalom would say he enjoyed relief from existence pain or, in Sartrean terms, his burden was eased of existential anguish, abandonment and despair. Now his life is an empty future without love, where he finds no good. This new life forced upon him is full of indifference and he feels sorrow and pain, and wishes for what he has lost: the love of his daughter and wife. He struggles to know if it is worth staying alive when the pain of life is so heavy a burden, his argument being that someone else chose to bring him into this world because they wanted him there and in doing so eased his existence pain. But since they have gone he bears his existence pain alone in a loveless life because nobody seeks his ongoing existence. So, what is he meant to do now?

Nevertheless, within the loving relationships he pines for he would still have felt existence pain, as we all do. The difference being, he would have shared such pain with his wife and daughter in loving them, and in their loving him.

It is when the beloved fails to ease the existence pain, and we theirs, that we tend to lash out. This becomes a spiral of conflict that many lovers find themselves in without knowing how they got there, why it continues and how to escape. This spiral is in the tragic duet *This is not Real Love* sung by George Michael and Mutya Buena. The couple were romantic lovers, but now he has withdrawn his romantic love because he believes she is about to withdraw hers. Their conflict is over an impending sense of aloneness they both feel will get worse when they finally split up, but nothing they can do will stop their going their separate ways, even though they promised it was forever when they fell in love.[62]

This song is a tragedy in the traditional sense as they both seek relief from existence pain, especially from being alone, and from one another, and yet he is reacting to an imagined belief that she is about to leave him. He looks for another beloved to avoid being alone and says she should do the same rather than hang on to him, even though abandoning her is the last thing he wants, and the last thing she wants too.

The song calls on both lovers to come together to ease their existence pain. Their love has helped them understand themselves as individuals and they sing of how their relationship used to be in intimate terms and how much they still need each another, but now they cannot break out of a spiral of destructive existential conflict. In the cold light of day, they need each other, but there is nobody to bang their heads together and tell them their existential conflict, despite uniting them, threatens their unity.

Beyond Existential Conflict

We have looked at two benefits sought by romantic lovers: understanding self and easement of existential angst (or existence pain). Most lovers find these benefits uniting, although they may cause destructive conflict. Lovers may seek other benefits through their relationship, but they must find a balance between selflessness and selfishness and a way to achieve the overall good they pursue. To do so they ask what they can gain, how much is reasonable and what they must sacrifice.

Without the achievement of the aggregated good in the three-pillar model — that being the total of the lover's good from the relationship — the emotional value the lover has become familiar with can drop away. If this happens, the immense value bestowed upon the beloved becomes difficult to maintain at a conscious level, because immense value is based on the lover's achievement of their good. The same can be said for the beloved, and if this happens to either the lover or the beloved (as a lover), the loving relationship is in jeopardy as the three-pillar model will fail if this pillar fails. Romantic love is a balance between selfishness and selflessness in pursuit of each lover's aggregated good, and many couples struggle with this aspect of love.

Meeting Secondary Conditions

As a lover you express needs, rights and values to your beloved through a collection of secondary conditions you expect the beloved to meet, but if they fail and you do not accept such failure, you withdraw your assured commitment to attend and tend, so that the commitment pillar fails and the loving relationship is ended.

In practice, there will be times the beloved will fail a significant condition, given that many are contradictory, conflict with deep-seated values, or could only be met by a saint. On failure you will feel the need to reappraise the beloved and the relationship to decide if you wish continue or end the relationship. If failure is your choice, you will withdraw your commitment to attend and tend by leaving the beloved, bringing the loving relationship to an end.

The most dramatized — although not necessarily the most commonly failed — secondary condition that brings about reappraisal is sexual fidelity, which is explored in depth in the 1987 movie *Fatal Attraction*. When Dan admits to a sexual affair with Alex, Beth, his wife, reappraises Dan and their relationship[63]. In doing so, she reviews several secondary conditions that support her assured commitment to attend and tend, such as love fidelity, sexual fidelity, honesty and selflessness. Dan also reappraises her as he too has secondary conditions.

He expects her to overcome failed conditions by pushing his infidelity outside her veil of assent or changing descriptors within, and wants her acceptance of his changing identity.

Like most couples in a similar situation, they reappraise one another by restating their conditions to themselves and to each other while maintaining their aim of achieving their individual good within the context of perfect-imperfect beloveds.

For many lovers, such significant condition failure as dramatized in *Fatal Attraction* is not a frequent event, but what all lovers do is experience the subtle background activity of maintaining secondary conditions where they navigate life together in the way Singer suggests. That is, love is an ongoing and subtle reappraisal whenever we feel frustrated, thwarted or weakened, or even gratified, fulfilled or strengthened. Where we feel frustrated, thwarted or weakened, we reappraise to determine if our good has been, is being and will be achieved in loving sentiment terms, and if the beloved remains our perfect-imperfect — and overall if our needs have been, are being and will be met. Moreover, we ask if our rights and values have been respected and will be in the future.

Reappraisal, whether brought on by a significant breach or ongoing background failures by the beloved, is not purely self-centred and we should sincerely hope the beloved achieves the same positive outcome in their ongoing appraisal as a lover in their own right. After all, the beloved seeks the good as we do and when they achieve it, we can, and when we do, they can within our community of two. As Singer says, secondary condition achievement and appraisal always include ongoing evaluations that embrace a view of a lover who really cares about the beloved and vice versa, although this happens in the context of love being a conditional affair. We all have ongoing needs, values and rights, and although we can and often do accept failed conditions, they should never be taken for granted as dramatized in *Fatal Attraction*.

Fidelity and Infidelity
Fidelity includes two intimately related secondary conditions. The first is fidelity of bestowed love (love fidelity) and the second is fidelity of sexual exclusivity (sexual fidelity). Looking at love fidelity first, in most romantic relationships a secondary condition exists where one or both lovers agree to bestow romantic love upon the other to the exclusion of all others. There are exceptions such as loving polygamous and polyandrous relationships, where a man has more than one beloved wife or a woman has more than one beloved husband. There are also open relationships where a loving wife or husband turns a blind eye or openly accepts their spouse's love of a mistress or lover or, in the absence of marriage, a lover accepts the same of their beloved.

Therefore a lover may take up one of two possible positions, either of which will be reflected in the secondary conditions of their love bestowed: either you cannot romantically love someone else and me at the same time, or you can romantically love someone else and me at the same time. The beloved's adherence to either of these conditions defines the success of the relationship with the lover. In setting down either of these secondary conditions, the lover accepts their beloved can bestow romantic love upon another person, and the beloved can rely upon the lover to continue to love them. Or the lover makes clear they will reject their beloved by withdrawing their love should the beloved take up a romantic relationship with another person.

In either case, fidelity is not entirely resolved. There needs to be an extended secondary condition set understood between lovers and their beloveds.

In a relationship where a beloved husband is barred from entering a romantic loving relationship with another woman, there remains the possibility of him having sex outside the marriage with his wife's blessing — unless his wife explicitly bars such activity through an extended secondary condition.

On the other hand, where a husband is not barred by his wife from bestowing romantic love upon another woman, he will probably engage in sex with his mistress, in which case his wife accepts both love infidelity and sexual infidelity.

In the first instance, the wife says "you cannot romantically love someone else and me at the same time" and either "you cannot engage in sex with anyone you choose and me at the same time" or "you can engage in sex with anyone you choose and me at the same time."

In the second instance, the wife says "you may romantically love someone else and me at the same time and I accept your love for someone else may include sex" and either "you may not engage in sex with anyone else you choose and me at the same time" or "you may engage in sex with anyone else you choose and me at the same time."

One of these expanded sets of conditions with the and/or resolved is applied during the bestowal of love. Should the beloved act outside of the secondary condition set laid down, this is reappraised by the lover (in these examples the wives), followed by one of three outcomes:

1. The original set will be reinforced with "promise… you won't do it again" followed by a restatement of the secondary condition set that continues to apply
2. The change in the situation will be accepted as a new state, followed by a clear statement of the secondary

       condition set that now applies
3. Love is withdrawn by the lover, and the relationship fails.

The acceptance of either of the secondary conditions that allows sex and/or romantic love outside of marriage is in conflict with mainstream Christian values. Nowadays, where secular and liberal values prevail, the tendency to break the secondary condition of fidelity is higher than in the past. We see this tendency, and the connection between love fidelity and sexual fidelity in *Fatal Attraction*.

When Dan tells Beth of his sexual affair with Alex, the first thing Beth needs to know is his loving status. He says that the affair was sexual only and that he does not love Alex. By distinguishing between sexual fidelity and love fidelity, Beth can understand where the secondary condition set failed and begin the process of reappraisal.

Selflessness and Selfishness

The objective of love when normalized is the possession of the good, that being the good life with the good beloved. And yet, achievement of this objective is not so simple as to ignore the beloved's achievement of their objective of love. Each uses the other as a means to their ends, even though to exploit and accept exploitation runs contrary to the fundamental morals of Western culture, where it is normal to reject anyone who takes advantage of you and vice versa. Exploitation between lovers is a little more complex. St. Augustine of Hippo in his essay *Morals of the Catholic Church* says you can view a beloved either selflessly or selfishly: the former is 'frui' and the latter 'uti'.[64] To understand both, consider a voyage on a ship. As a passenger, you can love the ship as a thing to be loved. Where she takes you and how she treats you on your voyage is not the basis of your love; she is simply a thing you bestow love upon because of her majesty. This is frui. On the other hand, the ship may feed you, shelter you and keep your glass full of what you like to drink as you party every night. Here the ship's importance to you is as a vehicle to your every whim. You love her as a means to your end as you would any ship in the fleet that does the same. This is uti.

St. Augustine argues that only frui is authentic love, particularly when it comes to the love of God given that his comments are in the context of religious *vertical philia*.

And yet you can view a beloved a third way, as a hybrid of frui and uti. You love the ship because she is that ship on that voyage. The voyage has no destination, as the purpose of travel is the voyage, of which she is an integral part.

Seen through these three lenses of frui, uti and hybrid, the lover can understand the nature of their exploitation, and moreover their beloved's exploitation of them. Therefore the lover can introduce any expected benefits that support their bestowal of love, at the same time accepting or at least appreciating any benefits included in their beloved's reciprocal bestowal of love upon them. With this in mind, lovers decide where their relationship lies —between uti and frui or in the hybrid centre.

A lover's bestowal may be based on the beloved as a woman adored in her own right, who deserves the good life she seeks at their expense and all benefits to them are purely accidental and irrelevant — although such love is questionable.

To another lover, bestowal may be based on their own ends, which may be a good lifestyle with a trophy beloved. Such a life may bring benefits to the beloved, but it is not essential. If making the beloved happy achieves the lover's own good, they will endeavour to do so, but only if it guarantees the lover's ongoing good.

Through the hybrid, a lover may bestow love upon the beloved to enjoy a good lifestyle with them, and them alone, in their own right. In this final example, the lover seeks the good lifestyle with the perfect-imperfect beloved who seeks the same: mutual good and a mutual good life. In this hybrid, the lover is not purely self-serving (uti), nor in pure adoration with no expectation of benefit now or in the future (frui). They seek a good life with that good beloved in their own right, which they know is achieved only through mutual good within a society of two, i.e. my good is created by your good, is created by my good, etc.

In any relationship, the lover may independently of their beloved see the beloved in frui, uti or hybrid terms, and the beloved may also see their lover in one of these three ways. In terms of uti, Bill Withers sings *Use Me.*, where the lover understands that his beloved uses him openly for her own ends, but accepts that and uses her too.[65]

Mutual exploitation does not exclude their reciprocal bestowed love when all three pillars are present. Above and beyond these will be the acceptance that this is a relationship of my beloved using me for her ends, and me using my beloved for mine.

Such a relationship may be considered inauthentic where the prevailing wisdom is that love in its essence is benevolent[XIII].

Authentic romantic love, as with all types of love, is defined by an ongoing bestowal of love against its three necessary conditions: recognised immense value in the beloved, assured commitment to attend and tend, and abstracted ownership of the perfect-imperfect beloved in the role cast by the lover. These three within the context of met secondary conditions between lovers or, where not met, accepted failure. So the lovers themselves define and accept all secondary conditions including any selfish characteristics of their relationship. On these points, love's authenticity is not debatable. In the 1955 movie musical *Guys and Dolls,* Adelaide and Nathan's exploitative loving relationship may be compared with Sky and Sarah's selfless one.

The musical tells the story of Sky and Sarah's falling in love relationship, in contrast to Nathan and Adelaide's loving one. Sky is a successful gambler and Sarah a Christian missionary working in a New York mission that reforms gamblers and alcoholics. Nathan is an unsuccessful gambler and Adelaide a singer and dancer. In the scene where Sky and Sarah return from Havana, Sarah confronts Sky after discovering her mission was used for gambling while she was away. She accuses Sky of manipulating her, concludes his intentions towards her are

---

[XIII] As Singer says, bestowed value [love] is different. It is created by the affirmative relationship itself, by the very act of responding favourably, giving an object emotional and pervasive importance regardless of its capacity to satisfy interests. Singer, I. *The Nature of Love – I Plato to Luther*, p. 5.

purely exploitative and breaks off their loving relationship as one of her secondary conditions is that this is a relationship where she does not use Sky for her own ends and Sky does not use her for his, particularly his gambling ends which she finds abhorrent.[66]

Adelaide and Nathan are more overt in what they seek from one another, especially Adelaide. From early in the movie, she tells him her dream to be in a normal relationship, with a normal husband, living a normal life, married with children and she sees Nathan as the one who will enable this for her.[67] This theme of her gaining benefit through her beloved plays throughout the movie and is stressed in two songs she sings in the club where she works.

In the first, *Pet Me, Poppa*, Adelaide plays a cat that tells her lover to pet her — not like stroking a cat at the fireside for comfort, but to pamper her with things like a cat that seeks its own benefit at your expense.[68]

The second is *Take Back Your Mink*. Adelaide plays a beloved whose lover recently attempted to seduce her after a five-year relationship which included him showering her with lavish gifts. As he seeks (one can only guess) sex with her she tells him — discarding the mink coat, dress, necklace and hat — to take back his gifts as she is not that sort of girl, suggesting she accepted them in the belief they were given out of benevolence. In her mind, he should not want anything in return for his love, especially satisfaction of a sexual nature, and in protest she wants nothing more to do with him. And yet, at the end of the song she reclaims the discarded gifts and asks the audience rhetorically if they would not do the same. This last point reaffirms Adelaide's message that using a lover to achieve her own ends is not only acceptable, but one should expect it, which is something Sarah would reject outright.[69]

Contrary to Singer's view, I believe that in all loving relationships there is an element of exploitation. He seems to argue that the bestowal of value, and with it love, is a benevolent act in itself.

Benevolence in love has two problems: the first is the

achievement of the good, where the good is the net benefit[XIV] you receive in your pursuit of love. When bestowing love upon your beloved you must accept, per Plato, that your bestowal is so as to be the recipient of the good within existence, i.e. the good life with the good beloved as beneficial to you. This life includes the romantic aspects of imaginative fusion with a soulmate in safe harbour, which relieve existential angst and create an environment between lovers of existential goodness. In these terms, romantic love has an uti underbelly where the lover's voyage is beneficial to self from the outset. Lovers such as Bill Withers skew their love towards overt exploitation and other lovers may skew their love towards the frui, similar to Sarah and Sky's love where benefits are less open. Nevertheless, in both instances there is predictable benefit in the decision to bestow romantic love that translates to the good.

The second problem in benevolence is that of avoiding the pain of not being with the beloved. Although emotional attachment is not necessarily universal, and not a necessary condition of love, I take the view, along with Singer, that love is an emotional endeavour as the three-pillar model suggests, so the emotional connection we create with the beloved can manifest as an attachment where to be physically apart is emotionally painful. For short periods we feel the emotional pain of limbic protest, and for extended periods such as breakups or death we feel the emotional pain of limbic despair. Both states are psychologically distressing as pointed out by Lewis, Amini and Lannon. The mix of emotions in these states can be agonizing, driving many lovers into clinical depression as Alex found in *Fatal Attraction* or even crazed suicide like Heathcliff in *Wuthering Heights*.[70] These extremes are usually found in romantic love, but feelings of loss are also found in the other loves when beloveds are absent for extended periods of time.

One might argue that avoidance of painful limbic protest or despair is not a benefit as nothing is gained and the anxiety

---

[XIV] Net benefit is determined by the lover when weighing up disbenefits versus benefits over time where on aggregate they believe benefits outweigh disbenefits.

brought on by thinking of pain is itself painful, which is not a benefit, but a disadvantage. But relief of pain, regardless of anxiety due to impending pain, is a benefit, where that pain and its anxiety are relieved by the assured presence of the beloved. For this reason, lovers take up abstracted ownership of their beloveds, many with great passion, as a means to secure their committed presence. With their presence assured, the lover gains relief from the anxiety of impending abandonment and avoids the pain of loss, whether that be limbic protest, despair or any other emotional hardship.

Both of these points challenge the idea of benevolence in the bestowal of love, and if the determination of future benefit is ascertained before the bestowal of love itself — as May argues, regarding hope for ontological rootedness on bestowal, and Plato, in pursuit of the good — then the decision to bestow love is inescapably founded on expected benefit.

Rejection of benevolence means that the bestowal of love is a selfish act, even when done with frui in mind.

And yet, although Wither's *Use Me* highlights the validity of a loving relationship of mutual exploitation, as short or long as it may last, love is bestowed by most lovers to connect to the beloved emotionally and vice versa, allowing both to gain benefit from their union on equal terms (or as equal as can be when considering the cultural background of equality between the sexes). By connecting through love, lovers can at least achieve self and joint-fulfilment that goes beyond giving and taking at a transactional level.

Honesty and Lies

It would seem all lovers should want honest relationships, yet many accept and often demand lies and where needed the omission of truth if it means their loving relationship remains intact. The notion that 'I would do anything for love' plays a significant role for many lovers. Some for instance accept that their beloveds engage in sex outside their relationship and allow for the lies that come with such behaviour, even where sexual infidelity breaks an overt secondary condition. Dishonesty can become so ingrained in some relationships that they fail without it.

Many examples dramatize such dishonesty, mostly because lies in the midst of love make great drama and the popular media idealizes a beloved who is honest, even though we know nobody ever is. In *Guys and Dolls*, Sarah expects absolute honesty from Sky because of her sense of Christian morality and the love ideal she has in mind of her romantic beloved, and yet in contrast Adelaide accepts Nathan is a gambler, along with the lies that come with his lifestyle.

Even more clearly than *Guys and Dolls*, *Lyin' Eyes* sung by the Eagles illustrates how blatant lying can be accepted within romantic love. The beloved loves a rich old man who fails to satisfy her sexually and strings along a poor younger man who does the opposite, but the old man knows she cheats and the young man knows she will never leave the old man because, as the title says, she cannot hide her lying eyes.[71]

The underlying point of this song is that if either man as her lover were to confront her, the outcome would be the end of the relationship — the unspoken lies are an essential part of the love dramatized.

Some might argue that her love is inauthentic and she uses one for his money, which the other cannot supply, and the other for their sexual prowess, which the first cannot achieve. These relationships are one-sided loves based on her exploitation, but let us not lose sight of the fact that both lovers accept their relationship as the only way they can love her, and on her part, she loves whom she chooses and where she finds the good.

It may be easy to dismiss *Guys and Dolls* and *Lyin' Eyes* as drama and say art does not imitate life, because many people may believe honesty should be a high secondary condition for all lovers. Yet conditions of truth are seldom part of romantic loving relationships. In all human interaction within and beyond the loving couple, lying is an essential part of daily life. Lies are not just statements of untruth; they are also purposeful omissions of facts best kept secret.

To expect a lover or beloved to be 100 per cent truthful would be an impossible ideal nobody could hope to achieve. Lovers accept — or rather expect within a healthy loving relationship — lies and held-back truths. This is because lying and holding back truths shield lovers from the gritty facts of being human and maintain the perfect-imperfect identity in support of each lover's ongoing possession of the good. So all lovers exchange an implicit agreement of sufficiency that supports lies and omissions as secrets and is integral to a loving relationship despite the danger between the fine line of sufficiency and the unacceptable. It takes lovers time to work this out, but each lover generally lies and remains secretive within their community of two.

Trust and Jealousy

Trust and jealousy play a significant role in the relationship between romantic lovers, which is not surprising given that the Western romantic love ideal demands sexual and love fidelity, while at the same time media bombards lovers with messages of sexual and love infidelity.

Specific to romantic love, the state of jealousy is present when:

1. The lover has already bestowed love upon their beloved, or the lover is close to bestowal
2. An interloper is present upon whom the beloved could well bestow their love, or already has bestowed their love
3. The lover believes the beloved is about to fail to bestow their love upon them, or is about to withdraw their love from them, because of their bestowal, or readiness to bestow, love upon the interloper.

In contrast, envy is a yearning for what another has. Envy usually involves two people and does not directly relate to the bestowal of love between them. Jealousy typically involves three people — lover, beloved (or potential beloved) and interloper — and directly relates to current or future bestowal or withdrawal of love by the lover.

Because jealousy includes the concern of losing the beloved, or potential beloved, to an interloper, it brings to the lover's mind the reasoned layer of the three-pillar model. The lover urgently asks: 'Do I possess the good, does the beloved achieve the secondary conditions of my love, and are they my perfect-imperfect?' If they conclude yes to all three, the lover will bestow their love to hold on to their beloved and fend off the interloper, or, if love is in place, reaffirm their love to do the same.

Jealousy is not always destructive. In fact, jealousy is an important ingredient of romantic love. It reveals to the lover that the underlying three predicates at the reasoned layer of the three-pillar model are in place, creating an opportunity for those falling in love to determine their readiness to bestow love, and for those already in love to consider the possibility of losing their beloved, and what such loss would mean.

The film *The Unbearable Lightness of Being* dramatizes this aspect of jealousy. After the dance, Tomas tells Tereza how sad he feels knowing she may be his friend's lover. Tereza teases, then dances with joy knowing his jealousy is proof of his love for her. Her reasoning is undeniable and they marry[72], so, destructive as jealousy may be, it can also act as a catalyst for lovers to realise their current position with their beloved. After all, as the saying goes, you don't know what you've got until you lose it. Jealousy, in Tomas' case, is the projected reality of loss that brings on realisation of Tereza's value — immense value as his beloved regarding the good he finds in her and his life with her.

However, jealousy becomes destructive when it includes an unshakable fear that the beloved has or will bestow their love upon an interloper, culminating in feelings of helplessness, frustrated anger, despair and, in extreme cases, rejection of the beloved out of hatred. In *Othello*, Othello smothers his beloved Desdemona because Iago, his trusted friend, manipulates his jealousy.

Shakespeare plays on a profoundly human theme: the underlying seed of distrust we all carry of our beloved who may love someone else instead of us. He nurtures this seed in Othello's mind in the first act of the play: '*Look to her, Moor, if thou hast eyes to see: She has deceived her father, and may thee,*' Desdemona's father says to Othello.

'My life upon her faith!' Othello replies in defence of his beloved.[73]

Although Othello's response is swift, the seed of distrust stirs in him and surfaces in the middle of the play when Iago tells him Cassio, once Othello's second in command, and Desdemona are lovers.[XV] Iago has no proof, but refers to Desdemona's father's earlier comment about deceit and embellishes his point by saying Venetian women have affairs and do not tell their husbands. He uses the word jealous, yet he is subtle in feeding the destructive nature of his master's jealousy. Othello, a foreigner, was unaware of Venetian women's affairs and his jealousy is evident when he says, alone and distressed *"Oh, that we can call these delicate creatures ours / and not their appetites?"*[74] Iago is exposing Othello to what we see every day as the media dramatizes how often men and women leave their lovers because of their sexual affairs, and Othello responds as any lover does when jealousy takes root. We take abstracted possession of our beloved by loving them with all our heart, mind, body, and soul. But no matter how we seek to bend them to our will we cannot stop them having affairs or loving others, where it is their nature.[XVI]

Iago finally convinces Othello by telling him Desdemona has given Cassio her handkerchief as a token of love. Othello presses him and Iago adds they are sleeping together. He leaves him to grapple with his love for his wife and moral disgust at her actions. At the beginning of the final act, Othello laments at her bedside, knowing he will kill her for being an untruthful adulteress as jealousy consumes him, contrasting with his idealization of her as his perfect-imperfect.

We sense his coming to terms with her dual identity when he uses the term strumpet, a whore, and yet, at her bedside he eulogises her perfection in life and death. He compares her

---

[XV] For those not familiar with the play, Othello is General of the Armies of Venice.

[XVI] The nature I refer to is reflected in popular media. If you listen to the penultimate verse of *Lyin' Eyes* by the Eagles you will notice how subliminally such nature may be broadcast.

complexion to smooth alabaster, the stone used to carve angels and saints in churches and graveyards. With this perfection in mind, he promises himself her death will not damage her aesthetic beauty through bruise, scar, deformation nor bloodstain.

In this speech, he moves her identity in life from that of perfect-imperfect to imperfect by bringing into his veil the adultery and lies that disgust him. Once in his veil, he purges these descriptors from her identity as it takes on the attribute of death to the point where he states he will love her as perfection through the purge of her disgusting deeds from her identity on her ascent to heaven. You see these mechanics of her changing identity when he tells her she must pray and seek absolution from God before he kills her or she will remain imperfect.[75] Through her death and absolution, he achieves the love he seeks of the perfect beloved — once she is dead. Nevertheless, through the destructive nature of jealousy, his beloved is gone, even if she is perfect in death.

One of the main secondary conditions laid down by lovers is the boundary between trust and jealousy. Lovers usually set this condition during the falling in love phase and of all the conditions, it tends to be one of the first tested, and it will continue to be tested throughout the relationship as lovers interact with the world beyond their community of two. As most lovers are monogamous in the West, where both sexual fidelity and love fidelity are expected, potential beloveds demand not to be put into a position of jealousy during their falling in love phase, and that condition carries over into being in love. This demands trust from both lovers at all times, although the potential for jealousy never abates entirely because of the sexual nature of romantic love. A beloved seeks faithfulness from their lover whom they know is driven by a similar desire for sex, while popular media circulates the beloved's desire for sex as irresistibly impulsive — what Othello refers to as '*appetites*'. When we are starving, we seek food and eat because we must without any thought of action and consequence — in other words 'I couldn't help myself; it just happened,' says the unfaithful beloved.

For most romantic loving couples, the shared secondary condition of 'Do not put me into a position of jealousy' stands above most others, while at the same time lovers remain in a quiet state of readiness — described as latent jealousy — to confront love infidelity the moment it is brought to consciousness. This potential jealousy, which lurks within the psyche of most lovers, was present in Othello, and is what Iago took advantage of for reasons unclear.

However, some couples embrace jealousy, as through it beloveds gain ardent proof of their lover's continued bestowal of love. For instance, the duet *How Blue Can You Get*, sung by Cyndi Lauper and Johnny Lang, portrays an enduring relationship where jealousy is central. The lyrics reveal a life of constant conflict, yet they have seven children[76] and the key point is this couple have implicitly agreed to ongoing secondary conditions of breakup and reunion through jealousy. Such jealousy proves their love is alive and passionate. They crave it, or rather the conflict it creates tears them apart and then draws them together passionately. For them, one of the secondary conditions of love is: if you are not jealous you are not in love with me, so prove your love with jealousy if you want my love to continue. The outcome for them is the passionately jealous perfect-imperfect lover.

So jealousy may be a constructive emotion that brings potential lovers together as in *The Unbearable Lightness of Being* although it came close to tearing Tomas and Tereza apart until they realised they must solve destructive jealousy with suppression and trust. For lovers like *Othello*, destructive jealousy causes anger, disgust and even murder. And for others like Lauper and Lang, tumultuous, clinging jealousy is an integral and passionate part of their ongoing loving relationship.

Maintaining the Perfect-Imperfect

Romantic love begins with two people who bestow love upon one another. In doing so, they embark on a journey of getting to know each other intimately while maintaining their perception of the perfect-imperfect in abstract ownership.

Of paramount importance during this phase of love is that

the lover's perception of the perfect-imperfect stays intact while the depth and breadth of the beloved are uncovered, and here is where potential conflict lies. The lover seeks the good, which they achieve in part by owning their good beloved whom they idealize to perfect, but the beloved is human and imperfect. There is a balance to be found between the beloved revealing enough depth of psyche and breadth of historical narrative of self to satisfy their lover's nagging curiosity of who they are, but they need to hold back enough to avoid tainting their identity in the lover's mind. The lover too wants to avoid poisoning their own mind by delving too deep into their beloved's psyche or knowing too much of their beloved's historical narrative; after all, lovers cannot leave outside their veil of assent everything uncovered about their beloved through this phase of love. Some things may be too significant to ignore. Lovers must learn to maintain their abstracted ownership of their perfect-imperfect beloved by digging far enough into their beloved's self to satisfy their need to know, and no more.

Psychological Depth and Breadth
Identity has two dimensions: depth of self and breadth of historical narrative, which accompanies that depth. If self is seen as a Russian doll comprising seven dolls, as you open each outer doll another smaller one is revealed which you can open until there are no more.

Using this analogy, the outermost doll of self is your aesthetic layer, the physical you. From a psychological perspective, this superficial layer gives you form and solidity in a world of things — of form and solidity that influence each other by cause and effect. Without this layer, you would not exist physically, nor would you be able to sense the world around you in terms of sight, taste, touch, hearing and smell or connect with the physical world.

The second inner layer of self is your presentation layer. This is how you present your psychological self through deeds and conversation, and interact generally so that people apply your aesthetic layer to your multifaceted personality creating your identity. People know you by the sum of everything you have done and said in the various roles presented through this layer. Without this layer, you would have no personality as your inner-psyche would have no means to interact with the outer real world.

The third inner layer of self is your perceptive layer, through which you perceive the world psychologically as sense experience. These senses include the five familiar ones of sight, smell, touch, taste and hearing, and many lesser-known ones such as the interoceptive sense of balance, the proprioceptive sense of position of body in space, and inner space senses of hunger, thirst and pain. Without the perceptive layer, there is no means to experience reality or perceive the needs of self, so that through this layer, you perceptively feel the outer space of reality and the inner space of self in relation to your physiological cravings.

The fourth inner layer of self is your limbic layer with which you psychologically sense the world around you. This layer is the seat of your intuition, where you sense the emotions of self and others or feel the void where there is an absence of emotional connection. These things are done through your limbic system, the specialised area of your brain that enables you to connect psychologically to the animate world around you, specifically people and other animals within the mammalian family such as dogs and cats. Without the limbic layer, you cannot connect emotionally with others through your presentation layer, feel sympathy or perceive the significance of your own and other people's emotional welfare, including loving sentiment, and would be as indifferent as a cold-blooded reptile.

The fifth inner layer is your memory layer, the most complex of all. Through this layer, you obtain, retain and protain[XVII] information that arrives from your perceptive and limbic layers. These functions support the cognitive and conative layers below that interact with the world through your presentation layer. For clarity: you collect (obtain) information from the world through

---

[XVII] Michael Inwood quotes Husserl's use of the term 'protain' when describing phenomenology and how we interact with objects in the world around us. Source: Inwood, M. *A Heidegger Dictionary*. 1999 Blackwell Publishers. pp. 162. ISBN 0-631-19094-5

your perceptive and limbic layers; you hold (retain) that information to process and inform; you predict (protain) by processing information. It is through obtain, retain and protain that you interact with the world at large on a physical and emotional real-time basis. At a deeper level, you also hold medium and long-term memory here, which informs you on past, current and future action so as to achieve all the benefits you seek. Without the memory layer, you could not process information or interact with the world to counteract imminent danger and fulfil current needs, and nor would you have a means of knowing self or anyone and anything else as a sum of your and their histories. You could not hold and execute strategies in support of your objective to possess the good you seek from the world at large.

The sixth inner layer of self is your cognitive layer, your seat of thought and conception where Reason resides. This layer receives information from your memory, limbic, perception and presentation layers, processes this information with the subsystem Reason and then interacts with the world at large through your presentation layer. Without this layer you would act on instinct alone, based on the subsystems of Fear, Desire and Thymos from your conative layer below and information from other layers above. You would do so with little conceptual understanding, strategic thought or moral agency.

The innermost layer of self is your conative layer, where unfettered thought percolates through the mind based on information from the layers above and subconscious background processing. This layer includes three subsystems: Fear, Desire and Thymos. Fear is never completely silenced, but is suppressed by your need to get on with life. Desire speaks unpredictably to you through cravings, but is usually tempered by your cognitive layer where Reason translates desires into strategies so as to acquire or deny you the things you want through moral agency. Thymos translates as the mind's passion for justice, dignity and value in terms of needs, rights and values.[77] For anyone who believes love to be unquenchable passion, this layer — and Thymos in particular — is the seat of love, where you feel the passion to fight and if need be die for love as well as dignity and justice. The conative layer is in constant tension with the cognitive layer as it makes demands for immediate action based on Fear's fear, Desire's desire and Thymos' passion for justice, dignity and value. Most of the time cognitive Reason constrains the conative from direct action, but sometimes the conative's Fear, Desire or Thymos win by directing the presentation layer to action.

This description of self is a simplified framework of the psyche to express the idea of depth.

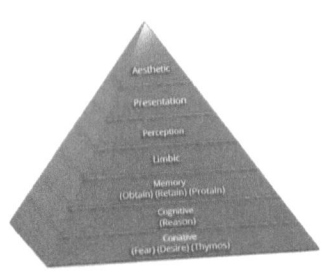

Regarding breadth of historical narrative, consider the framework as a pyramid, with seven horizontal strips top to bottom as depicted. The strip at the top is your aesthetic and your conative fills the bottom with all other layers progressively filling the horizontals. You present yourself to the world in a very narrow way with your aesthetic, but as you make your way down the layers more depth of self is exposed, depending on how deeply you wish to share with those around you. More breadth of self is exposed depending on how much of the narrative you reveal.

For instance, you would not expose yourself beyond your presentation layer to a stranger, but to a romantic beloved, especially within a long relationship, you might offer much deeper insights, sharing intimate memories and including the narrative with them, and you would expect your beloved to share theirs with you. As deeper layers of self, such as desires and passions from your conative layer, are exposed, you might limit their breadth to what you feel comfortable with. At our most intimate level, we feel uncomfortable revealing uncontrolled thoughts of desire and despair as well as the emotional narratives we would only share with those of highest trust, if at all.

Since romantic love tends to be intimate, lovers expect their beloveds to open themselves up in psychological depth and breadth. They seek this for three reasons:

1. In a beloved sharing psychological depth and breadth, lovers gain a keen sense of who their beloved is. These shared thoughts offer surety that they have found the good beloved and the good life they seek.
2. The act of loving is emotionally active, not sterile, or passive. As beloveds expose depth to their lovers, the lovers seek the underlying narrative in breadth from the beloved. They need this to connect emotionally with meaning to their beloved — or, as Lewis and his co-writers would argue, to limbicly resonate.
3. Through sharing both depth and breadth, lovers create trust which eases points of potential conflict in the pursuit of good, maintenance of the perfect-imperfect identity and negotiation of conflicting secondary conditions.

For these three reasons, many lovers demand exposure of depth and breadth from their beloveds.

But we must temper our sharing and seeking of depth and breadth of identity as by knowing too much of our beloved, irreversible pollution of the perfect-imperfect may occur — although by knowing too little we struggle to know and trust them.

In the 2004 movie *We Don't Live Here Anymore*, the balance of too much and too little emotional depth and breadth is extremely difficult for the lovers to work out and maintain. The film tells the story of Jack and Terry's struggling marriage. Jack is having a secret romantic affair and to avoid the guilt of leaving Terry, he wants her to withdraw her love and leave him, so he manipulates her into having a sexual affair with their friend Hank. This presents a part of Jack's psyche that brings about conflict after her first sexual encounter with Hank, when Terry explains how she struggles to understand Jack who presents a base desire from what seems his conative layer for her to have sex with another man, and yet no breadth as to why.[78] She concludes the benefit Jack seeks is that of sexual satisfaction when he really wants her withdrawal of love. Since the former is driven from the conative layer and the latter the cognitive, she receives conflicting signals and does not understand why he is rejecting her within the broader context, which she has sensed for some time as well as his absence of jealousy.

In the pyramid diagram, as Jack pushes Terry away in the first half of the film to make her withdraw her love, he reduces his depth and breadth of psyche to her up the pyramid. This is what Terry reacts to in the bedroom scene when she says she would rather be at home than with Hank, but she is confused because Jack is purposely misdirecting her as he wishes her to sleep with Hank. He shows signs of jealousy, which he quickly suppresses when she tries to see the depth and breadth of his psyche because he knows that to know him deeper and broader will ruin his plan to drive her away.

We see depth and breadth of identity in more clarity when Terry arrives home after her second time with Hank. She cannot understand why he should hate her when in reality he refuses to know her, and she claims his view of her based on what she does and not who she is is not valid. She says that Jack's identity as a whole, now and in the future, is him, not merely what he does,[79] and that lovers build an identity of their beloved based on who the beloved is as much as what they do. By saying this she infers that the beloved expresses themself in the depth and breadth of their psyche beyond their aesthetic and presentation layers and that lovers love souls not actors.

This movie shows the need for lovers to expose emotional depth and breadth to support love's ongoing bestowal. Terry cannot understand who Jack is because he obscures his depth and breadth, and Jack refuses to see Terry in the psychological depth and breadth she would like to share with him. These are the reasons their relationship is failing.

Yet lovers should not know everything about the beloved's psyche. Were Jack and Terry not fictional, would they survive as a couple reconciled beyond the credits? Has either of them too much knowledge in depth and breadth of the other? Has either perfect-imperfect identity been damaged irreparably, regardless of the veil of assent and Stradivarius effect?

The phase of being in love is centred on discovery. Lovers must learn to love, which includes learning to use their veil of assent and the Stradivarius effect effectively. Beloveds must learn what to share with their lovers if they wish to hold on to them — too little depth and breadth and they may be an untrusted stranger, too much and they may become an imperfect-imperfect.

Chapter 9

Romantic – Staying in Love

The two notable elements of romantic relationships within the phase of staying in love are familiarity and trust, which create a firm belief in the perfect-imperfect beloved for each lover, forming communities of two that rarely break apart. This phase of staying in love is seen in couples who have spent many years together and who share many of the following traits:

- ♥ A history of good times and bad that bind the couple together as a community of two
- ♥ A sense of closure for significant conflicts of the past, and few expected in the future
- ♥ Any remaining points of conflict found in falling and being in love are set aside, and love and sexual infidelity become less of a concern because trust is higher than in earlier phases of love
- ♥ Children are older and seek independence if they are not already independent, and there may be grandchildren
- ♥ The intensity of life slows as the lovers are less caught up in the rat race
- ♥ Sickness and dependence upon either beloved is an increasing risk
- ♥ Death threatens their community of two.

This gives context to this phase of love, summed up in The Beatles' song *The Two of Us* as having more memories than road ahead.[80] The lovers' attitudes are skewed towards past sentiment, and they feel connected to each other by years of shared history.

This leaning backwards to the past contrasts with the falling in love and being in love phases of love, which are both dominated by present and future sentiment. The staying in love phase is one of robust togetherness where the past binds lovers.

Woody Allen's 1986 film *Hannah and Her Sisters* offers deeper insight into staying in love over three key sequences covering events in Hannah's family between two Thanksgiving celebrations hosted at her parents' home in New York.

The first opens with Evan, Hannah's father, playing the piano during the first Thanksgiving celebration while Norma, her mother, sits opposite him and they sing *Bewitched, Bothered and Bewildered* from the Broadway musical *Pal Joey*. Their extended family gather round and listen as they revel in a trip down memory lane surrounded by objects they treasure, particularly old photographs of themselves and the family.[81]

In the next scene Hannah comes home to resolve an argument between her parents. Some of the usual romantic friction points of love relationships are revealed — infidelity, selfishness, lies and jealousy. These secondary conditions, the hardest for romantic lovers to deal with, define romantic love. Illustrating these conditions shows how this phase of love raises the lovers above their history. In Hannah's brilliant monologue[XVIII], she betrays her parents' turbulent past and how they all survived.[82]

Although infidelities, selfishness, lies and jealousy contradict their nostalgic view, the lovers look back and value their numerous conflicts through shared past sentiment because of their sense of comradeship and the way they have dealt with conflict and survived together with the continual revision of their secondary conditions. Allen evokes a sense of perverse romanticised struggle between Evan and Norma.

This sense of nostalgia based on conflict is not unusual. War veterans who fought on opposite sides often see themselves and each other as victims of the same war and not as enemies.

In the final sequence, Evan and Norma are at the piano once more and it is the following Thanksgiving. The camera pans the

---

[XVIII] Applied as the camera pans the apartment again of the couple's treasured objects and photographs.

room full of extended family and memorabilia[83], showing that both Evan and Norma are at relative peace against the backdrop of the tempestuous history that brought them together and holds them there.

The 1981 movie *On Golden Pond* offers deeper insight into a couple's final phase of love as they approach the end of their lives:

Norman and Ethel, now retired, spend the summer at their Golden Pond home as they have done each year throughout their marriage. They argue over their age, their past, her choice of him as her beloved, his health and dying — all dominant themes of staying in love, which are replayed throughout the film. Norman worries about memory loss, but feels safe with Ethel in the face of encroaching dementia. His vulnerability and dependence bring about a strengthened community of two, where attend and tend are an active element of their love.[84]

In relation to perfect-imperfection, Norman is grumpy, argumentative and insufferable. This attitude strains his relationship with his daughter, Chelsea, which the film sets out to resolve. Ethel remains steadfast in her perception of him as her perfect-imperfect beloved and is happy in her perfect-imperfect life with him. Norman feels the same about her and the community of two that sets them apart, even if this means their child sees herself as an outsider.[85] This sense of looking in at the couple from the outside is reflected in Hannah's monologue when she describes her parents' relationship, which has grown stronger with age.

As Norman and Ethel pack to leave, he falls ill, but although Ethel thinks he is going to die she is not frightened.[86]

She reflects that lovers who love at this time of life are mindful of their beloved's ailments and impending demise. They know they will live on, holding on to the memories of their lives together until they themselves die. Here the good held will become nostalgia once grief is less crushing.

Staying in love is for lovers who have been together for a long, but indefinable time. The lovers' lives are slowing down, many of their conflicts are resolved and their bond is strengthened through their community of two as their children become independent and leave home. The lovers tend to rely on past sentiment since their past is an interwoven narrative of their good, but, they seldom forget they fought side by side — and at times with one another. Their shared narrative is also proof that the present and future is and will be peacefully good and the beloved they now know intimately is their perfect-imperfect. The lovers are also aware that as a community of two they will depend increasingly on one another. They understand their own mortality and that one may die before the other, but this does not mean the future is bleak, just that sickness and death are inevitable and so lovers must make the most of what they have and take what comes in their stride.

Part 3
Animate Love

It is good to love as much as one can, for therein lies true strength, and he who loves much does much and is capable of much, and that which is done with love is well done.

—VINCENT VAN GOGH[87]

Chapter 10

Romantic Intimacy Not Included

The animate loves deny the romantic intimacy that defines romantic love. They include the love of people in roles cast by the lover whether they be self, mother, daughter, brother, grandmother, pet, friend or society as a whole. These are in sharp contrast to romantic love, where we find one type of love only.

Chapter 11

Self Love

Self love begins with an idealized idea of the perfect beloved, in this case, self, followed by appraisal and bestowal of love upon self. Such bestowal is based on assured commitment to attend and tend as with any bestowal of love, and a sense of abstracted ownership.

Love is bestowed upon self in the same way as any beloved, insomuch as self is considered a second party. This is done because you find good in life with self, you fulfil your own needs, accept your own moral and ethical shortcomings and consider self a good person in perfect-imperfect terms.

There are two crucial aspects of self love:

1. Appreciation of oneself through a sense of self-identity
2. Appraisal of that self against a preconceived ideal of the perfect self.

These are followed by the bestowal of love upon oneself where the perfect-imperfect is perceived.

Appreciation of Oneself as a Self-identity
The person you see in the mirror is not your total self; that physical reflection is just one small part of you. It is the physical and psychological being that make up the self. Your physical self includes tangible features specific to you such as qualities of body shape, proportion and symmetry as well as specific interactive attributes like posture, mannerisms and gait — how you present and move your body. This part of self is easy to recognize and understand when you stand in front of a mirror or walk past a reflective shop window.

The greater part of self is more difficult to understand, as it cannot be seen in direct reflection. This is psychological depth and breadth.

Together these two distinct and discrete parts of self, the body and inner-psyche, create a greater whole, perceived as identity.

Identity has three perspectives: real-identity, others-identity and self-identity.

Real-identity

You have inherited your nationality, race and family heritage, matured as a physical and emotional person, done things, been places, met people, been affiliated with religious and political groups, felt and shared emotions, owned possessions, shared thoughts and aspirations, and loved and hated people, things and ideals.

Your voyage of real-identity began on the day of your conception, and ever since you have collected more and more descriptors without ever dropping earlier ones. The voyage continues and you add descriptors until your real-identity solidifies to an unchanging set of information the day you die. Your real-identity cannot be changed by anyone, including yourself. It is simply a mass of unbiased historical information specific to you that roots the physical you to the past and present.

Others-identity

Similar to your real-identity, others-identity is a list of historical descriptors specific to the physical you that each individual who knows or knows of you holds in their mind.

These unique others-identities are called identity mosaics, where each identity mosaic of you includes:

- ♥ Your aesthetic, deeds and shared thoughts to date
- ♥ All accepted descriptors from others who know of you
- ♥ What they imagine you could do in the future.

Everyone who holds a mosaic of you also has embedded within it their judgement of your past deeds, shared thoughts and physical self. Such judgements — based on the moral importance of descriptors relating to your history — are applied to their mosaic of you. The result is that some descriptors take a more prominent place than others with high importance descriptors dominating your mosaic and obscuring lesser ones.

To complete the mosaic, related descriptors are clustered together, setting out what is in effect a relational databank specific to you and you alone. The result is that as they recall one descriptor they tend to remember other descriptors within the same cluster too, prioritized by importance.

Self-identity

Self-identity differs from real-identity and others-identity insomuch it is a single self-constructed view of self. Like the others, it includes descriptors of your body and past deeds, but also your perceived inner-psyche.

The mosaic shown is a tiny part of my own self-identity mosaic, which includes what I know of my self based on what others have told me, but with self-moderated importance and clusters applied.

Like an ancient Roman floor mosaic made of thousands of individually shaped tesserae, overriding attributes of my self-identity are clear from a few feet away due to the clusters of large letters, descriptors and their importance. Up close the detail is more granular, where small, related groups of tesserae reveal finer detail. This overarching fine detail is the identity I know myself to have.

Your self-identity mosaic, like mine, is the result of years of reflection by many people. Without reflections of yourself from others you would have no way of knowing yourself in totality.

This inability to know self, particularly in a psychological way without other people, is due to two phenomena:

1. You have no means of stepping outside self to examine self in depth and breadth

2. The importance and clusters of descriptors presented to you are a result of other people's judgements. In your mind, those people agree collectively, if you choose to allow them, on what is morally right and wrong, and aesthetically pleasing and displeasing about you. You can understand these phenomena through a simple thought experiment:

If a child — let us call her Tars-Anne — matures to adulthood alone in the jungle will she know what is right and wrong and ugly and beautiful? It may be true she would have a basic idea of self as something that takes what it wants to achieve its good, but self-identity would be extremely limited in descriptors, clusters and importance. This limitation of knowing self is because we apply clusters and importance based on what others think about past deeds, shared thoughts and physical aesthetics. Simplified and in the absence of other opinions, morality and beauty are meaningless to Tars-Anne.

In understanding self-identity as a reflection from other people with your own moderated clusters and importance applied, it is evident that love of self reduces to a belief you are worthy of your own love based on self-identity. Here love is bestowed upon self by comparing yourself to your ideal of perfection, and that perfection is whom you would like to be in terms of someone high in moral agency and aesthetic. And yet in this summation we find a problem that must be solved.

Two parts of self-identity must be remedied before you can appraise self to an ideal of perfection, or in loving terms perfect-imperfection. The first is the slanted reflection of your identity from other people. The second is that you cannot deny truth, which usually tips self-identity towards the negative. You cannot pretend that the wrongs you have committed are not wrong, in the same way you cannot say the sky is green when you know it is blue.

Descriptors of others-identity mosaics will always be skewed one way or another, either through important and densely clustered descriptors because people believe you have done or said good or bad things, or because you may be affiliated with a religious, ideological or racial group that they like or object to. Polly Nelson, Ted Bundy's defence attorney before his execution in 1989, had a distorted view of identity when she said he was "...*the very definition of heartless evil*"[88] when he committed abduction, rape, murder and necrophilia.

Stephen Michaud said in his book *The Only Living Witness: The True Account of Homicidal Insanity* that Bundy concluded he was a cold-hearted son of a bitch.[89] This view of self could only be because other people reflected the descriptor of heartless. As a psychology graduate, Bundy knew that to be heartless and evil is also to act without guilt, and do things generally considered to be morally wrong.[90] In the absence of other people's reflections of his psychological self, he would never have known that almost everyone has a sense of guilt that guides them to do right. He acknowledged as much when he said how fortunate he was not to be troubled by the pain of guilt.'[91]

As well as taking on the negative descriptors of cold-hearted and guiltless, Bundy also accepted son of a bitch, which has two meanings he must have understood: the first referred to his illegitimacy — his father left soon after he was conceived[92] — and the second refers to his historical narrative of forcing people to do as he wanted. Confessing to crimes of abduction, rape, murder and profanation led to his execution.

Bundy is an example of someone taking descriptors into his self-identity mosaic and applying other people's importance and clusters, or at least their sense of right and wrong. The result is a skewed view of self, based on other people's sense of morality.

Beyond psychological identity, people also slant aesthetic identity. The media celebrates physical beauty while drawing a parallel between physical unattractiveness and low morality. These messages create a correlating perception that beautiful people are healthy, good and sometimes smart, as they think and do beautiful things, but everyone else tends to be unhealthy and act immorally.

In Victor Hugo's novel *The Hunchback of Notre Dame*, the physically disfigured Quasimodo is described as having low morality and no intelligence. His thoughts are *atrophied* by his physical deformity, Hugo writes. He goes on to say, "*The reflection which resulted from this refraction was, necessarily, divergent and perverted,*"[93] referring to Quasimodo's perception of the world and meaning that the world is clear through our well-formed eyes, but Quasimodo's world is perverted by his. The logic is that if you can only see evil, you must be evil.

In the 1988 movie, the crowd crowns Quasimodo King of Fools at the foot of the Notre Dame bell tower for his grotesqueness. Everyone but Esmeralda finds him ugly, a fool, dangerous and feral.[94]

When he visits Esmeralda in the bell tower, he shows that he has absorbed other people's descriptors by telling her not to come close or look at him as he is neither a man nor an animal, but an ugly savage.[95]

These are particularly negative cases of psychological and aesthetic reflections of self-identity, but there are always despairing people who present a distorted negative reflection and try to force you to do what they want out of envy or because they cannot influence you. In your steadfastness, their biased reflection tries to make you obey them by changing who you are, what you do, how you look and even whether you exist. Some people present a skewed positive reflection of you — possibly because they have no reason to do otherwise, or have a relationship with you they value, or they love and admire you as someone of wisdom and virtue.

Perhaps they want to help you overcome a negative psychological bias of your identity, which you find painful, and even harmful.

An array of reflections of self from others, negative and positive, will build and maintain a balanced self-identity mosaic. Negative descriptors weigh you down, and descriptors already present may change with importance and drag you into the negative too, but sometimes positive descriptors will be added or importance increased so as to lighten the load. In this, self-identity is an ever-changing feature of self.

This happens in the 2015 movie *Angel-A,* where André is saved from self-destruction by an angel (Angela) when he replaces self-loathing with self love. Angela helps him achieve this by presenting herself as him and reflecting his self back to him in a way he can accept and love.

At first, he is confused — she is female and he is male, so how can she be his reflection? How can he trust any reflection of himself? She tells him he has a feminine interior with sensibility, humour and wit, but his masculine traits have held him back and are pulling him down — that he needs to see himself in a new light.[96] It is only through a new reflection that he can understand who he is as an entire identity and begin the process of appraisal against a preconceived ideal, followed by bestowal of love upon self.

The underlying question is, can André believe what she tells him about self, especially knowing the past deeds, psyche and physical aesthetic included in his current self-identity mosaic?

If I were to tell you a lie, you would not know it was a lie without my admitting it, although I would. The fact I know the truth gives me an especial depth and breadth of knowledge of self. Your own attributes, deeds and thoughts can become negative descriptors of your self-identity if you believe immorality or ugliness lie.

No matter how hard you try to forget or deny these private negative descriptors, you cannot. You are forced to accept your history of doing wrong and thinking wrong, and that your body is not aesthetically beautiful.

If these private, negative descriptors are high in importance and cluster, it becomes difficult to accept positive descriptors as reflections of self from other people, especially when such self-known negative descriptors dominate your identity mosaic. The result is you have no means to love self because self is not worthy of such bestowal. In fact, the only way you can escape the negative descriptors of self is to become worthy of your own love by:

1. Pushing negative descriptors outside your veil of assent knowing they do not relate to self as a function of your perfect-imperfect and then applying the Stradivarius affect to create the perfect-imperfect that match your ideal identity
2. Elevating important positive descriptors to

overshadow negative ones, and then applying the Stradivarius affect to create the perfect-imperfect that match your ideal identity

3. Replacing your current identity with one you consider ideal.

You can use any one of these options in full or a mixture of 1 and 2, first to create a self-identity of the perfect-imperfect self, then match this to a preconceived ideal of perfection. Once this has been achieved, you are ready to bestow love upon self.

Appraisal of Self to a Preconceived Ideal

Like all love types, you appraise the beloved against a preconceived ideal to determine the presence of the perfect. For self love, the ideal will be the person you aspire to be, who will give you the good life you pursue. And the beloved is self, who knows you inside and out, and whom, in turn, you know inside and out. Once you have an idea of the ideal, you ask yourself how to achieve it and to love yourself. At this point you choose from the three options: one and two remedy the mismatch between your self-identity and the ideal you strive for by using the veil of ascent and Stradivarius effect and modifying your behaviour and maybe appearance. Option three allows you to believe that you are the ideal by wholeheartedly taking on the identity of the ideal you seek to be. The differences are subtle but substantial. We see the latter in the 1992 movie *Single White Female* and the former in *Angel-A*.

In *Single White Female*, after Allie's lover leaves her, she takes in Ellen as a roommate. Unbeknown to Allie, Ellen is psychologically unstable and takes Allie's identity, which she considers to be an ideal identity. This becomes clear as Ellen starts to dress like Allie and copies her hair colour and style. Then she looks in the mirror and professes her love of self as she takes on her new identity,[97] but her love fails as the reality of the situation between her and Allie progresses.

Ellen lays out her struggle to love self in this way in a suicide letter she has Allie write. She concludes that she does not need a reason to kill herself, she needs a reason not to. Even though the letter is meant to be from Allie, it is actually Ellen's, and relays her feelings about her self-identity.[98] In fact, her conclusion could be André's in *Angel-A*, or Francis' in *Exotica*. None of the three can love their selves without changing their self-identity.

In Ellen's case, the underlying problem in loving self is that out of the three ways to love self she can only manage the third: to replace current identity with a new idealized one. Such a replacement is only possible through delusion under a psychological condition because self-identity as a function of one's history in deeds, thoughts and aesthetics cannot be denied by a healthy mind.

For a healthy mind, we first look to others to help define an ideal self-identity, but do not adopt that identity. Instead, we create a set of attributes from what we learn from heroes, film stars, media personalities, athletes, friends and family for whatever reason we find them morally or aesthetically appealing. These attributes offer a sense of the person to aspire to, perhaps someone we do not want to disappoint. You may say you want to live up to your father's aspirations or your mother's, a friend's or God's. For aesthetics, you may want to look like this model or that movie star or pop singer. Some people want to be thin, fat, muscular or busty, and others are just happy as they are.

Once the ideal of self is developed, in terms of a set of moral and/or aesthetic attributes we would like to see in self-identity, we seek to change self-identity to align to the ideal. We do this through the veil of assent, the Stradivarius effect or by changing our lifestyle to be a better person ethically, or even by changing our appearance with cosmetics, clothing, diet, prosthetics or surgery. In this way we accept we can never be the ideal, but only strive towards the ideal as a perfect-imperfect person.

Angel-A dramatizes the alignment of the self-identity mosaic to the ideal of self-identity. Standing in front of a mirror, Angela tells André to bestow love upon himself. She says he deserves such bestowal after she has shown him through the movie that he is ethically and morally a good man. He struggles with her idea of deservedness, but with hindsight and a new perspective he decides he can love himself.

André is not delusional in his bestowal of love. Unlike Ellen, he has not rejected his identity for an idealized one. He knows his bestowal includes imperfection for his past poor moral judgement in thought and deed, and imperfection of aesthetics, so his love of self is based on his use of the veil of assent and Stradivarius effect.[99]

These two movies show that to love self you must appraise self to an ideal. That ideal is either an entity in full, at which point you are ready to love, or an ideal as a set of values taken from others, which may include a view of aesthetics, so that you compare the ideal to your self-identity and then embark on change, which may consist of modifying your aesthetic and/or behaviour to become a perfect-imperfect person good enough to bestow love upon. You also amend your veil of assent and Stradivarius effect, and the result creates the conditions to take up abstracted ownership of self in readiness for love's bestowal. This is actually insufficient for love's bestowal as the other two pillars of assured commitment and value are not in place, but it is sufficient for the attachment pillar.

The next question for the lover is "Do I gain the good with self?" If so, immense value is bestowed upon self and the value pillar is put in place in readiness for this aspect of love's bestowal. When Ellen and André are satisfied in identity, they also feel a sense of wellbeing. Their wellbeing translates to a sense of achieved good now and in the future. By achieving this, they construct the value pillar and bestow immense value upon self. This is not always true as life's outlook tends to be more extensive, but your view of self as good, and how you perceive your ability to gain your good now and in the future plays a significant part in your determination of self-value.

The final aspect of love's bestowal upon self is assured commitment, and particularly the secondary conditions that support such assurance to self. In *Angel-A,* André is in a state of self-loathing at the beginning of the film, about to end his life because he cannot bring himself to love himself and only through Angela does he come to terms with his broken conditions, which fail his needs, rights and values. She helps by getting him to use his veil of assent and Stradivarius effect successfully, and by dropping troubling conditions through modifying his ideal of self. Once this has been achieved he commits to attend and to tend to his self and not disintegrate.

With all three pillars in place, love can be bestowed upon self. In André's case, he looks in the mirror and says he loves self. Ellen does the same in *Single White Female*. We tend to be less explicit, but when bestowing love upon self, the three pillars must be in place for Love to span them. And where one fails, love fails.

Chapter 12

Family Love

The traditional view of the nuclear family is a man and woman within wedlock and their genetic children, and demonstrates four types of love:

- ♥ A mother's love for her children (maternal)
- ♥ A father's love for his children (paternal)
- ♥ A child's love for their parents (filial[XIX])
- ♥ A brother and sister's love for each other (sibling).

This tradition goes beyond the nuclear family to the extended family of grandparents, grandchildren, nephews, nieces, uncles, aunts and cousins, all genetically connected and loving. Such a view of the genetically related nuclear and extended family raises the question of whether there is any difference between strong and weak genetically bound families in terms of loving relationships?

The answer is in the traditional family. In the song *Dance with My Father,* Luther Vandross reminisces about his filial nuclear family where he, his mother and his father all loved one another.[100] This sounds like the ideal family because the shared sentiment idealizes the traditional genetically bound family based on pre-20th-century Christian family values when anything else was unconventional. And yet, was this ever the norm across the West? I do not know of a study looking into whether the nuclear family was ever widespread, but what we do know is

---

[XIX] Where there is genetic connection, filial is the correct term for this love type, however it is better described as child love — lifting it from genetics to broader love that encompasses the role of parent and son or daughter regardless of genetics.

that such idealized families hardly existed by the mid-20th-century.

The 1948 Kinsey Report on the sexual behaviour of American men claimed that the traditional nuclear family held together by genetic relationships was not so prevalent, considering the number of sexual partners in and out of marriage and sexual infidelity practised across American society. Kinsey's conclusion was backed up by a second similar study of American women four years later[101] and there is no reason to believe that anything has changed, nor that this only applies to America. Divorce is more frequent now than during the late 1940s and affects huge numbers of dependent children in single-parent and remarried families,[xx] as well as common-law families and families with fostered and adopted children which are now commonplace.

Vandross' song need not be sung by a genetically related child for the love depicted to be authentic even though romanticism conjures up images of such tightly bound perfect families. Genetic links are not a direct factor in loving relationships between family members, but genetics may be used as a secondary condition of love's bestowal. If a father has a secondary condition of loving his daughter, his bestowal of love may be withheld or withdrawn on discovering she is not genetically his, although another father may not hold such a secondary condition of paternity and continue to love his daughter regardless. The same may be true for extended members of the family with no genetic links.

Therefore family love has little to do with the traditional family ideal of genetic inheritance between family members. At a fundamental level, all loving relationships within family love are the same as any other type of loving relationship and include the

---

[xx] According to the UK Office for National Statistics 2012, the divorce rate had increased from ~5% in 1950 to ~10% by 2012 with close to 50% of divorces affecting children under 16 years of age. Furthermore, as divorce rates have increased in the UK over the past 65 years, marriage rates have dropped, suggesting an increase in common-law relationships. These include same-sex common-law relationships too, after the legitimisation and common acceptance of same-sex relationships in England, Scotland and Wales. Referenced: http://www.ons.gov.uk/ons/dcp171778_351693.pdf sourced August 2015.

bestowal of immense value upon the beloved, abstracted ownership of the beloved and assured commitment to attend and tend to the beloved. This remains true while the lover achieves the good they seek to hold onto, the beloved remains the perfect-imperfect, and the lover's secondary conditions remain satisfied. For some lovers this may include a genetic connection, but genetics are not a universal demand.

Parental Love

You may believe that a parent's love is instinctive and unconditional, but this is not so. Three other primary factors beyond genetics support or deny a parent's bestowal of love upon their child:

1. Family duty
2. Family role
3. Lover's good.

Family Duty

There is a direct link between benefits expected by a child and family duties placed upon the child by the parent in exchange for those benefits. This exchange is the underlying nature of all tightknit social relationships and can be seen most vividly in parental love. Such a link is because children, especially younger children, actively seek parental love as a means to ease their existence pain in terms of:

- ♥ A realisation of the inevitability of their, and in the background their parent's, death
- ♥ Their ultimate aloneness beyond the nuclear family
- ♥ Their freedom to act without the wisdom to make wise decisions
- ♥ The absence of any obvious meaning or sense to their lives.

To remedy such existence pain, children look to each parent for safe harbour in a hostile world. They seek support in avoiding the indifference of life that comes when alone and help in coping with an unpredictable reality that, for the most part, does not bend to their will. In exchange, most parents demand of each child certain behaviours and duties that are bound to family responsibility. Where the child does not meet these demands, a parent may choose to withdraw their bestowed love so that the child must meet the parent's needs, respect their rights and/or match their values. Where they fail, they fail in their duty to the family by dishonouring the parent.

Madonna's *Papa Don't Preach* outlines the desperation of a daughter who believes she has failed in her family duties and fears her father's withdrawal of love, having discovered she is pregnant and intending to keep the child and marry the father. She seeks her father's forgiveness, blessing and the assurance he will continue to love her even though he disapproves of the relationship.

If her father accepts her failed duties — those of remaining chaste or at least avoiding pregnancy out of wedlock, and marrying a man he does not approve of — he will continue to love her. Otherwise he will withdraw his bestowed love.[102]

Papa Don't Preach highlights the situation where secondary conditions of a parent's love include family duties. Where children fail in their duties, bestowed love is reappraised and perhaps withdrawn.

Most parents forgive their younger children who are unable to make sound decisions that fail duties, but some immature, irrational children who fail secondary conditions are held responsible in the same way Madonna describes.

Dave Pelzer's novel *A Child Called 'It'* depicts his youth as an abused child. When he was eight his mother withdrew her love in the belief he was a bad child who could do no good. His frustration and devaluation from a human being are reflected in the book's title.

Pelzer suggests his mother's psychological instability and addiction to alcohol were the underlying reasons for her hatred of him, and this may be so if you consider love irrational and that her alcohol addiction and mental health problems suppressed a natural bestowal of love. However he recognises love is rational when he repeats that he felt no love from her when she was lucid and sober and not depressed, and that she was affectionate towards his three brothers and her husband.

An eight-year-old with little understanding of family duties would not rationally choose to revolt, but this made no difference to his mother's withdrawal of love. Although he had no means to regain her love, that did not matter to her either, regardless of a child's understanding of conditional love.

Family Role
>Jaques:
>*All the World's a stage,*
>*And all the men and women merely players;*
>*They have their exits and their entrances;*
>*And one man in his time plays many parts...* [103]

Jaques' lines are from Shakespeare's comedy *As You Like It*. He says that from the moment we are born until we die we are taught to accept the fundamental idea of role-playing so that the roles become so ingrained they are second nature to us.

The list of roles is endless — police officer, teacher, pilot, bank teller, doctor, nanny, professor, zookeeper, soldier, waiter, street cleaner, writer, politician, vicar, school child, prisoner, terrorist, bank robber and kidnapper — and they are all defined by title, rights, duties, deeds and shared thoughts. The roles we adopt are not limited to profession or pastime, they cover all aspects of life. In family roles we see mother, brother, father, son, uncle, cousin, grandfather and so on as discrete titles with similar obligations.

Some people embrace these varied roles, while others avoid them and the relationships and bestowals of love that arise from them. A father may reject his daughter for either a non-genetic connection or failed duty on her part and refuse to adopt his normal duties, deeds and attitude by refusing to act as her father.

The 2000 movie *Duets* tells the converging stories of six people who have lost their ways in life, but together find meaning through a karaoke contest. Ricky and Liv's story is about a father's reluctance to bestow love upon his daughter, not because he doubts paternity or failed duty on her side, but because he refuses to accept the role and duties of a father. He refuses when he finds out he is her father, even though she recognises him at once and seeks a loving father/daughter relationship.[104] The point of their story is Liv's desire for him to accept his role, which will enable her to love him.

Out of frustration, Liv finally rejects him wondering why he will not acknowledge her as his daughter — intimating his rejection of role — and tells him she feels sorry for him because she finds his pity for her denigrating, and she refuses to be belittled by not being loved by her father.[105]

Because of Ricky's refusal to take up the role expected of him, he has no basis upon which to bestow love when he is ready to do so. This is true for all types of love. The love object — Liv in this case — in their role as perceived by the lover is the basis upon which love is bestowed. For instance, if Ricky had befriended Liv he would have a basis of platonic friendship upon which to bestow his love and if he took her on as a romantic beloved, he could bestow love on that basis. However Liv is Ricky's daughter and, if he accepts he is her father, he can bestow love once the three pillars are in place, which he does at the end of the film.

This is crucial in understanding love as it shows that love is role-based. We love beloveds in a role, and consider ourselves within a role as we do so. Our role as a lover may be benign — for loves that are not interpersonal — but within the family the lover's role is as vital as the beloved's.

Lover's Good

After genetic relationships, family duty and the family role, the final primary factor of parental love is the expected good of the parent.

The objective of love is a lover's possession of the good, or the perfect life with the perfect beloved when idealized. This may be based on uti, frui or hybrid — where bestowed love is uti based, the lover seeks their own good with little thought of their beloved's good, but where bestowed love is founded on frui, the lover seeks no good, or solely the beloved's good.

Regarding parental love, in uti relationships the exploitation by the parent of the child is the basis of the relationship.

Conversely, for frui relationships the parent accepts the exploitation of self by the child wholeheartedly, as the child's good is the good they seek in achieving their own good. Such love is sacrificial and often seen when the child is very young. As the child matures, frui based parental love may change to a hybrid or uti relationship as the child becomes less dependent on the parent, less demanding and less selfish. As this happens and the child becomes emotionally mature, a parent's expectation of reciprocation grows stronger.

In uti based parental relationships from the outset where a parent's good fails to materialize, they withdraw their love, or have never bestowed it. This is not to say that a parent who loves in terms of uti avoids legal and moral duties associated with the provider, but that they will not bestow love upon their child until they feel they achieve their good, which may not be until the child is old enough to offer rational benefits or reciprocation in kind — or never at all.

This can be seen in the films *Mind the Gap* (2004) and *A.I. Artificial Intelligence* (2001). The former tells the story of five people seeking happiness. Malissa was conceived by rape and her dying mother has found no good in life, which she blames on Malissa's unwanted conception. Although she has dutifully brought Malissa up regardless of absent love, she tells her how much she hates her, and it seems her child could never have offered her anything towards her good as a basis to be loved.[106]

A.I. Artificial Intelligence examines the situation of a mother who withdraws her love from an artificial child who perceives her as his loving mother. The premise is whether a mother can love a robot that is human in all but in nuance, though not organically or genetically. The broader question is what the expected good she may seek from an artificial son by loving him when he loves her, and how this compares with the expected good a mother may seek from a real son in loving him when he loves her.[107]

David is a gift to Monica five years after her genetic son, Martin, goes into a coma. When Martin recovers David accidentally endangers him and Monica, realising she should return David to the factory for destruction, abandons him in woodland.

In the absence of her own son, Monica has used David to fill the emotional void. After his abandonment David asks if his mother loved him and could he be loved again if he can make up for what led to his abandonment. He concludes he was loved and that the remedy is to be a real boy like Martin, and he rejects the idea that people love out of benefit.[108]

Joe, a robot David meets in the woodland, rejects David's conclusions, believing that robots, even those who act as loving children, are loved only when they offer their owners benefit. Where benefit — the good — is absent for the lover, love is not bestowed, or is withdrawn when the good is lost.

This example is extreme as David is artificial, a tool, and like any tool made for a purpose. Where the purpose is not met, perceived value is low. This value is reflected in Joe's rejection of David's argument, who thinks he is not loved because he has failed to meet the expectations of the user, Monica. Although the situation is fiction, there are instances where parents conceive children for a specific purpose and rejection may follow the failed purpose.

A mother may have a daughter to hold on to her beloved husband, and love her for it, but if her husband leaves anyway she may reject the daughter. Or a father may love a son in the belief he will achieve immortality by his son carrying on the family business or continuing the genetic line. If his son rejects the company or decides not to have children, the father may withdraw his love. Parents may have children for a specific reason and love them on these terms, because some lovers base their good on a particular benefit or set of benefits.

Finding the good and holding on to it in raising children tends to be subtler than these fictitious examples, nevertheless we should be mindful that parental love, like all love, has an element of possessing the good.

♥

Beyond the four primary factors of parental love, other

considerations force parents to evaluate their relationships with their children. A parent must consider all conditions if they are to bestow and maintain their love, although many parents contend that their love for their children is unconditional.

In some relationships, unconditionality is weak, so something trivial may result in a parent's reappraisal, followed by their withdrawal of love. In other relationships, the withdrawal of love's bestowal only happens under extreme circumstances. This is when loving sentiment at the emotional layer is so strong that virtually nothing the child can do could bring about rejection. Here unconditionality is strong, but love is never completely unconditional. Reappraisal is always in the background for failed conditions by a child or unsatisfied good expected by the parent.

Child Love

Child love, as opposed to parental love, includes the four primary factors of:

- ♥ A genetic relationship with the parent or caregiver
- ♥ The perception of the parents' acceptance of role and duties
- ♥ The acceptance of their role as daughter or son
- ♥ The expected good the child seeks to gain and maintain from their bestowal of love.

Again the adjective/verb problem of love distinguishes between feelings and the conscious bestowal of love, and the difference between these two related but separate aspects is most visible in child love.

Thinkers and philosophers make the case that human behaviour is learned apart from some simple animalistic actions.[XXI] If so, we are taught how to love as this is not in our genes, and it is at this point that we separate the verb to love as something learned and the adjective of feeling love as an

---

[XXI] Sartre makes the case in *Being and Nothingness* that human nature — the nature of people above their nature as animals — is not as extensive as many people believe, and argues that everything we do except for some very basic animalistic functions, is learned.

instinctual way of feeling, especially regarding early childhood development.

Harry Harlow, the respected American psychologist, studied early life development of higher primates over many years, including humans. He concluded that their psychological development covers five discrete steps in their progress towards maturity.[109] This process begins with the maternal love of the child by the mother and the child's innate response to that maternal love as the momentary satisfaction of its needs. Four steps follow this innate response[XXII]:

- ♥ Infant love towards the child's parents or surrogates (child love as an adjective begins in infancy and develops towards late childhood in learning the verb of love)
- ♥ Peer love (sibling and friend love, from late childhood through adolescence)
- ♥ Heterosexual love (romantic love — Harlow uses the term heterosexual, but in today's terms this should be 'agnostic of sexual preference')
- ♥ Paternal love (parental, extended and social love, including the now adult child's children, and extending from the family to the extended family and society in general).

Both innate response and infant love manifest as a limbic connection between mother or caregiver and baby and are the start of a journey of discovery into love. As the child matures with loving sentiment in the background, it learns from experience how to emotionally connect with its parent in a meaningful way. This connection results in its informed bestowal of love upon its parent and those around it when old enough to consciously do so within the three-pillar model.

Harlow says that the five steps are all necessary and sequential within healthy development. When one step is missed or poorly applied, the child struggles to accept and reciprocate

---

[XXII] I have mapped each step to the love types described in this book.

love as an adult.

Harlow's five steps and the three-pillar model show the transition between a child saying they love their parent in an adjective way, and the bestowal of love in a verb way. Until the child knows what bestowal is, they will only articulate what they feel. This implies children cannot love until they have the ability to connect emotionally with others and apply the three-pillar model. We learn to feel love as an adjective, followed by learning to love as a verb when we are able to choose whom to love.

This view of a child choosing not to love their parents contradicts popular opinion, but the difference is down to the adjective/verb problem. When a young child says I love you, Mummy, or I love you, Daddy, they say what they feel, but an older child will say the same as they bestow their love within the three-pillar model.

Whether that is an innate response, infant love, or the child's feelings overall does not reduce the importance of love as an adjective. This variant of love supports a meaningful relationship between a parent and their child and as Harlow states the feelings commonly called love are precursors to the rational loving relationships the child will experience later in life.

Genetic Relationship

As the bestowal of love by the child is a conscious choice, the genetic connection between child and parent has no bearing on love's bestowal unless the child chooses to make this a condition. Nonetheless, there is an affinity between many children and their genetic parents. This genetic affinity may form the basis of a loving relationship if the child chooses to pursue love with their parent.

The 2016 film, *Lion* tells the story of Saroo who is driven to find and reunite with his genetic mother after a separation of 25 years. When he finds her, he contacts his adoptive mother and father and tells them that his newfound relationship with his maternal mother does not change his feelings for them. He loves them and although his mother is now in his life he still considers them his mother and father too.[110]

This illustrates that a genetic relationship between child and parent is not necessary for love's bestowal but, where one is present, a feeling of affinity is enough to begin appraisal of a genetic parent with the aim of building a loving relationship should the lover choose. This film also shows that there are no limits to the number of parents loved when it comes to child love.

Perception of Parental Role and Duties

The parental role and related performance of duties by the parent are essential elements of child love. Failure to take on the parental role of a father, for example, also brings about the failure of fatherly duties, so that the child struggles to bestow child love upon the father while the parent denies them the status of daughter or son — and the perfect-imperfect beloved to own in abstract.

Although the uptake of parental role and duties are linked, they can be separated.

Returning to *Duets*, Liv wants to love her father, but finds it difficult to bestow her love upon him since Ricky refuses to take up this role and rejects parental duties. She has always fantasized about having a loving father and loving him in return, but Ricky refuses to acknowledge the role of father so as to avoid the duties of fatherhood. Liv persuades him to take up his duties of assured commitment to attend and tend as her mother did as her means of loving him, where he is there should she need him — which is closer to friendship than the traditional daughter/father relationship Ricky had expected. Once he understands this and accepts the duties of the relationship, he takes up his role as father followed by his bestowal of love, which comes with an assurance to attend and tend.[111]

This shows how a parent's role rejection can affect a child's ability and desire to bestow love upon their parent. In contrast, the 2009 film *Precious* shows a young woman's struggle with a parent who takes up their role but neglects their duties. Her parent abuses her sexually, physically and mentally until she refuses to bestow love upon them.

At the end of the film Precious' mother asks her to come

home with her newborn son (and brother) and explains why her father had abused her sexually from an early age. Her mother not only accepted this, but added her own deliberate and vindictive physical, mental and sexual abuse. The family implodes because of this history of failed parental duty.

Precious decides not to bestow love upon her mother and explains that while she may have been stupid in the past or in denial, she never wants to see her mother again and leaves her pleading.[112] Precious recognises her mother did not fulfil a mother's duties and did not protect her from her father's abuse. As a child, she had no free will in her mother's charge, but as an adult she is free. She chooses to leave and deny her mother of her love, based on her mother's past failure to meet her maternal duties.

Child's Role and Duties

To create a child love relationship a daughter or son must accept their role and its duties.

We Need to Talk About Kevin (2011) is about a son's relationship with his mother, where he pushes her away purposefully from an early age and rejects the duties of his role, and ultimately the role itself, denying himself love without knowing why.

Kevin believes the pointless act of repudiating her through rejecting role and duties is of little consequence, denying his love for her in the same way a parent denies their love for a child when they reject their role and duties as a parent — as in *Duets* before Ricky accepts his role and duties as father. Not until later does he realize no act is pointless, by which time he cannot love the one who wanted to love him the most: his mother.[113]

This movie depicts psychologically troubled Kevin, while showing that a child's love cannot develop if they refuse to take on the role and duties of a son or daughter and play the child's role. In saying this, they deny their ability to love their parent as they now have no parent, and also deny the parent their love as their parent loses their son or daughter as a love object.

Lover's Good

At first glance, and in contrast to parental love, the general view of child love is an uti based relationship where the child takes and the parent gives. Such a view is based on the Western social attitude that a parent's love should be unconditionally strong, probably because in the early years parents nurture their children, which is mostly giving.

However when children grow up and mature emotionally, they learn to bestow their love in pursuit of their good and understand their beloved's needs in gaining their good too, so there is no reason to apply uti stereotypes to child loving relationships.

In relationships where children bestow their love on an uti basis, parents give accordingly and where a parent fails, love may be withdrawn. Like all loving relationships, each child loving relationship is distinct and conditional regarding the lover's good.

Sibling Love

Sibling love offers many benefits to lovers, and genetic relationships, roles and duties play a similar part in sibling love as in parental and child love.

Modern families' genetic relationships are diverse, and loving relationships between filial, half-filial and non-filial siblings are complicated, although a genetic connection does not necessarily have a bearing on love's bestowal.

Sibling roles depend on the roles and duties performed by parents, caregivers and other siblings. A neglectful mother leaves a gap where an elder or dominant sister may take on her role and duties, although siblings may not accept her in a motherly role even if she is forced to adopt one. In effect the sister may have two roles: sister and mother, the latter without the title, but with the authority and duties that come with the role, and the former with the title, but somewhat resented for the authority she wields.

As the motherly sister matures, her mothering role will be reflected in all her loving relationships as expected in Social

Cognitive Theory.[XXIII]

Other factors of sibling love beyond genetics, role and duties are jealousy, trust and envy. The delicate balance between jealousy and trust is not exclusive to romantic love. They are active elements when siblings compete for the love of others — especially their parents, but also others within and beyond the family.

Envy is also an active element in sibling love when siblings compare themselves to each other and make a loved value judgment — *if you have more than me, you are loved more than me*. This is not jealousy — here, one sibling believes they are loved less, so wants what the other has — love, or more of it.

Role and duties

Woody Allen's *Hannah and Her Sisters*, a film of many dimensions, dramatizes the roles and duties taken on by three siblings and the loves between them and those around them.[114]

Hannah is older than her two sisters, Lee and Holly. Their parents have focused on their own careers and their tumultuous loving relationship, with the girls left mostly to fend for themselves. Consequently, Hannah stepped into a matriarchal role in the absence of her mother. In doing so, she took on the attributes of sibling and de facto mother. The matriarchal role adopted by Hannah so early in her life is reflected in her marriage and the attitude her husband, Elliot, has towards her, and in the relationships she has with her younger siblings. Elliot finds her too giving and, in response to this, seeks somebody to whom he can give too. Her sisters, especially Holly, look to her instead of their mother for support, which overwhelms Hannah at times.

This phenomenon of the role-based relationship and the duties it brings between loving siblings is a strong theme in sibling love. With it come many challenges for siblings to love

---

[XXIII] Albert Bandura, a professor at Stanford University, laid down the principles of what is known today as social learning and social cognitive theory. He has published many books and papers on the subject, the most notable being *Social Learning Theory* (1997) and *Social Foundations of Thought and Action: A Social Cognitive Theory* (1986).

one another, given that attitudes to a role often change over time, whilst the expected duties of a role tend to stay the same.

In a practical sense, Hannah's sisters view her as a sister, even though they expect her to stay on matriarch duty in perpetuity. Furthermore, Hannah herself suffers from the same problem. She has taken on the duties of a matriarch towards Lee, Holly, her mother, her father and Elliot for so long she finds it difficult, if not impossible, to release herself from this de facto role. Throughout the movie her siblings bestow love on the secondary conditions of: *remain our matriarch* and *support us as we think our mother should*. And yet when it suits they expect her to be able to drop into an equal role of sibling, rejecting her matriarch domination.

Envy, Jealousy and Trust
Within tight-knit family relationships, envy, jealousy and trust tend to be common destructive themes. The most famous siblings who struggled with them were Cain and Abel in *The Old Testament*, the sons of Adam and Eve. Cain, the firstborn, was a farmer and Abel a shepherd, but God had 'respect' for Abel and his offerings, but none for Cain.

Did Cain kill Abel because he was jealous, envious or both? Siblings may compete for the love of others, especially their parents' or caregivers', and siblings may be envious of one another, both of which set sibling love apart from other interpersonal love types. In romantic love for example, envy is usually suppressed as romantic lovers each tend to celebrate the good of the other. In the same love type, jealousy is balanced with trust in the presence of loving sentiment. In friendship love, these traits are usually concealed as friends seldom compete with one another in a romantic sense out of respect for the friendship. They also avoid competing for non-romantic goods without looking to resolve conflict amicably first. In their envy and jealousy, sibling lovers are closer to companions than any other love type. Companions choose cooperation to compete with other people, but one will take what the other cannot have if the stakes are high enough and this usually destroys the companionship. However, blood is thicker than water, and for the family's sake siblings tend to reconcile eventually.

Role, duties, envy, trust and jealousy are defining factors of sibling love, all set against a contemporary context of changing family makeup including secular views on marriage, common-law and same-sex relationships, and sexual equality.

Extended Family Love

Where sexual interest, shared interests, values or common beliefs bring people outside the family into your life, the roles of grandfather and grandmother, grandchild, uncle, aunt and cousin do the same. Once in your life, you choose to love them or not based on their role, and performance, and they do the same.

Like all loves, the necessary conditions are founded on immense value, assured commitment to attend and tend, and abstracted ownership of the perfect-imperfect role, although of the three pillars, abstracted ownership of the perfect-imperfect role is the most significant aspect of extended family love, because the role forms the basis upon which the relationship is built.

When you love your grandfather, there is little doubt he is your perfect-imperfect grandfather, even though he is as imperfect as any man may be. What is important to you is that in his role of grandfather he is the perfect-imperfect grandfather once all preferred attributes of grandfatherness are within your veil, all non-preferred attributes that are not a part of grandfatherness remain outside your veil, and you apply the Stradivarius effect. When you run this across the extended family, love is the possession of the perfect-imperfect grandfather, aunt, cousin, etc.

We love extended family members because each accepts and performs their duties within their roles. Each role defines the person and many of the secondary conditions that come with love between extended family members. A grandchild will love their grandfather under the secondary condition *as my grandfather who acts like one and treats me as a granddaughter I bestow my love upon you*. The grandfather will love his granddaughter under the secondary condition *as my granddaughter who acts like one and treats me as a grandfather I bestow my love upon you.* The roles are played out by trial and error as we communicate our expectations through Social Cognitive Theory.

Adoption of the extended family role and its duties brings us to the romantic taboo. There is disapproval even where no genetic connection exists between lovers or where a genetic link has little bearing on reproduction. Where a family member has a role, they have duties within that role that exclude romantic relationships with other family members.

In the 1987 movie *Flowers in the Attic*, Corrine marries and has four children with her father's half-brother. After his death in a road accident, she returns to the family home with the children hoping to win back her dying father's love but, enraged with Christian piety, Corrine's mother discards her role of grandmother to the four children, offering them only food and shelter. She is undeniably their genetic grandmother, but she will not take on the role or duties of grandmother, nor bestow love upon the children.[115] Therefore the grandchildren do not love her because she denies her role and duties.

In the media, separation of extended family roles and romantic love is reflected as a cultural norm. Nieces, cousins, adopted relations, step-relations, etc., include platonic relationships where romantic loving relationships are considered taboo and incestuous. When a romantic relationship occurs, lovers are shunned regardless of any bloodline between them.

When lovers remain together in spite of being ostracized, they drop their extended family roles and duties and adopt their romantic lover role as lovers, since this role dominates. They seldom forget their original extended family roles beyond the relationship, as these bind them historically to their family and hold them there when they are not rejected, but when together as lovers they are romantic lovers.

Animal Love

When it comes to loving an animal, as a separate species there should be no barriers to love's bestowal. The necessary conditions of love are your bestowal of immense value, assured commitment to attend and tend and abstracted ownership. Where these are present you know the good you achieve and possess is present; you have your secondary conditions of love satisfied and you recognise your beloved as your perfect-imperfect in the role cast. However, when we love we tend to enjoy a physically close and emotional relationship with the beloved, and in the case of an animal the secondary conditions of needs, rights and values bound to physical closeness to the beloved raise broader questions: is it only pets that we love because we can get close to them or does loving an animal make them a pet by virtue of the lover's emotional relationship with them?

In general, a pet is a tame companion for our pleasure, which suggests we are physically close to it without danger of harm to self. If the animal can eat, bite or sting you, you cannot get close enough to create an emotional bond.

Physical closeness to a pet creates companionship or pleasure at the emotional level of the three-pillar model because of limbic connectivity and resonance which are strong factors in physically close relationships. And yet limbic connectivity, resonance or physical contact in pursuit of companionship are not necessary conditions of love.

Pen pals and prisoners may bestow love from afar, and people who have never met fall in love over near-instant media such as text or email, where imagination bridges the physical gap. Their love is as authentic and, in cases of romantic love, as romantically intimate as people who bestow love within a physically close relationship.

The tame aspect of loving may therefore be disregarded as it is not relevant in loving an animal. You may love a domestic dog or cat that you are physically close to, or a wild animal where your respect for its wildness at a distance becomes an essential factor in your love. Researchers on the African savannah bestow their love on one, several or all lions in a pride, and so do crocodile keepers who know they are not safe in the water with their wild beloveds.

Companionship or pleasure derived from the beloved is a deeper question of the good gained from the bestowed love.

In the 2011 film *War Horse*, Albert takes on the difficult task of training a stallion, Joey, to work the family's failing farm. He appraises Joey and, without mentioning it, bestows his love. When World War One is declared Albert's father sells Joey to the British Army. The groom scolds Albert as he says goodbye to Joey, believing it is okay to love a dog, but not a horse, which raises an important distinction in the unequal love of animals as it suggests that a beast of burden is neither a pet nor an object of love since its use is solely exploitative and thus the antithesis of an idealized beloved.

Albert accepts that Joey is a beast of burden and must earn his keep, but he is also an admired comrade and a member of the farm — within the commune, within the family. In this combined belief, the lover accepts the beloved as perfect-imperfect within the dual roles, where one is equal and the other is unequal. This duality is an important factor for the bestowal of this type of love as it allows the lover to change their view of the beloved as equal in some situations and master/slave in others.

Lovers take up a posture of protecting the welfare of their dual-role beloveds as a means to hold on to the good they are and offer. This means the lover's commitment to their beloved ensures they are not placed in a position where they are devalued, harmed or lost outside the relationship, even in situations where others can see the beloved in a master/slave context. This is why Albert is comforted with the promise that Joey will be cared for by the captain who will take him into battle while surprised by the groom who berates him for treating a horse like a loved pet.[116]

Therefore the love of an animal like Joey or a domestic pet such as your cat or dog or a wild lion is as valid as any other love type. There are no barriers to the necessary conditions of love when it comes to animals. As with all loves, animal love is reasoned. The lover seeks to achieve the good, have their secondary conditions satisfied, and see within the beloved the perfect-imperfect in the role cast. In the case of Albert, he accepts Joey as a working animal and at the same time places him as an equal so that Joey takes on comrade status, and Albert forges a loving relationship that brings about his own good.

This ability to love animals comes about because all three necessary conditions of love can be met by the lover against the three-pillar model. Yet this raises another question: animals cannot love you in the same way you love them, so how can your love be authentic in such a one-way relationship?

There is no necessary condition of reciprocation between lover and beloved. There are interpersonal loves where reciprocation is sought, but this is not necessary for love's bestowal. Romantic in-love, for example, requires reciprocation, but infatuated and delusional romantic love does not. Friend loves are dysfunctional without reciprocation, but love *per se* is not dependent on this. The fact an animal cannot reciprocate your love with conscious bestowal is no barrier to your loving it.

Many species, particularly domesticated mammals such as dogs and cats, present human-like emotions amongst themselves and towards us. These emotions can be perceived as love in the adjective sense and many people think of their animal's behaviour as love. But such displays of emotion and behaviour are not a bestowal of love within the three-pillar model.

Dogs may show limbic protest and despair when separated from their owners, but a dog cannot rationally bestow love upon its owner based on satisfied needs, rights and values in any meaningful way or withdraw such bestowal on failed conditions, one of which might be *you always leave me lonely when you're gone*. Its limbic system deprives it of reward in your absence, making it feel limbic protest as it howls and paces back and forth in distress, and the same applies when you arrive home and it jumps all over you in greeting, but limbic satisfaction and protest differ from love as a rational bestowal.

This does not diminish the loving relationship you have with your beloved. Dogs can be loyal companions and cats can curl up on your lap and keep you company when it is cold. Horses can take you where you want to go without asking why, and people who work with wild animals say that each one has a personality of its own that makes it unique and loveable to them.

Chapter 13

Friend Love

There are three types of friend love: companionship, friendship and comradeship, although this often causes confusion as many consider friend love to be a single type of love: friendship. However there are distinct differences.

Plato's view of love is possession of the good. The *Symposium* states that the lover ultimately seeks the possession of the highest good, which is ascension on death to an overworld alongside the Godhead. To Plato, this is a place of immersion in beauty for eternity for the lover, who takes on beauty in spirit and possesses beauty by becoming all-knowing in the same way as the Godhead. To acquire this highest good, the lover must embark on the *scala amoris*,[117] a lifelong journey of differing loving relationships, one of those being pederasty, a specific kind of friendship love.

Pederasty is viewed today with cynicism as it represents a relationship, usually sexual in nature, between an older man and a juvenile boy, but Plato rejected the sexual nature of the relationship and saw it as infusing the beloved boy as he matures with wisdom and virtue only.[XXIV] By loving in this way, the two lovers travel a road of constant learning and teaching together. When the elder lover dies, he knows that his search for wise and ardent virtue will be continued by the beloved boy, who pursues the struggle for wisdom and virtue with a young beloved of his own once he too takes up the *scala amoris*. Plato's friendship love is an eternal relay of attained highest good for ongoing

---

[XXIV] Virtue is one of the defining attributes of friend love. It is to know what is right and wrong in the sense of societal laws, norms and customs, and to consistently and predictably do right, even where that results in failure to achieve a benefit sought for self.

generations,[xxv] and he considered pederasty the most genuine of loves within the bond of friendship love.

Fifty years later, Aristotle approached friend love from a different angle. He gave three reasons lovers enter into friendly relationships in the first place: goodness, usefulness and pleasure of the beloved. He viewed a relationship based on goodness as a perfect friendship, one where the lover seeks the good for the beloved and the beloved seeks the same for the lover, neither expecting the good in return.[118]

When we compare Plato and Aristotle's theories of friendship, we understand why people bond, the context in which love is bestowed, and the types of love created on bestowal. Interpersonal relationships begin with acquaintance and develop through emotional depth and breadth. Aristotle claims that when two people find each other to be of equal virtue, and seek the good for one another in shared virtue, their relationship becomes a friendship love through bestowal.

However, where they find and accept self-sought advantage in each other but, like friends, seek the good for the other as a general rule — the relationship will be one of platonic companionship.

Beyond Plato and Aristotle, when people are thrust together out of necessity in a situation of shared do-or-die, they may seek advantage in each other and accept advantage sought from themselves. Thrust together in this way they may find they share no values — in fact, outside their situation of do-or-die they may well dislike one another, but they cooperate to survive, and bestow their love upon one another for the duration of the situation as comrades.

Finally, two people who find pleasure alone in a friendly relationship and hold back from emotional depth and breadth will be detached friends without bestowal of love. They will

---

[xxv] There is a clear distinction in terms of the Athenian practice of pederasteia and Pandemotic Love. In the former, the older lover views his protégé in terms of Uranian Love, focusing on the boy's soul as he teaches him wisdom and virtue. In the latter, the older lover focuses on the protégé's aesthetic beauty in terms of satisfaction of sexual desire. This is the distinction Plato draws regarding friendship love.

remain aloof in their emotionally shallow understanding of each other. These friends keep in touch, but are not within each other's inner circle.

Companion Love

Companions enjoy their shared experience and express robust concern for each other on their journey of joint and self-improvement, but they accept a degree of exploitation from each other and, should the need arise, one will ultimately take what the other wants and then leave. Friends do not do this. They stay together where possible and avoid exploiting each other. They walk side by side, seeking the good for one another and accepting it with no explicit expectation of benefit, although they do strive to hold on to their individual good. Companions also walk side-by-side but compete with the world, one with shield, the other sword, striving towards goal after goal as a community of two. They do so for as long as each achieves success. If a goal is established that only one can reach, they will separate from the community of two to attain it, leaving the companionship behind.

This self-serving conclusion does not mean a companion lover would deny their beloved the good they seek or their success. Companions support each other where they do not compete, but they may compete for something they want of higher value than the companionship itself.

Companions seldom contend to the point of companionship failure, but fight and defend as a community of two for scarce resources and status, and horse-trade minor benefits only one can enjoy. If one of the beloveds oversteps the mark and takes or achieves something they shouldn't, the other rejects them and the relationship founders. Where a lover climbs politically higher than their beloved for example, inequity sets in, or where a companion takes a romantic lover whom the other companion wants, there may be envy and mistrust. In these circumstances, conflict follows and the companionship may end abruptly.

This does not invalidate companionship in terms of love and satisfaction. Like friends, companions feel enormous sentiment for their beloveds gained through deep, broad, emotional relationships. The difference between friends and companions is not of limited depth and breadth or mismatched values, but of secondary conditions associated with love bestowed, particularly: *I expect to benefit from you within and beyond this companionship* and *I accept your exploitation of me up to a point within and beyond this relationship.*

By adopting this secondary condition of love's bestowal, the beloved understands that love is companion-based and accepts that the relationship is one of mutual benefit as well as of mutual exploitation where and when the need arises, and may founder as a consequence. The challenge for both lovers is in understanding where the line of unacceptable exploitation lies. If you overstep the mark, your beloved may withdraw their love, leaving you both bitter and alone as you feel the need to account for your behaviour to a beloved who now considers you exploitative for using them for your own ends. They feel especially used when they thought themselves and the relationship of higher value than you did.

In the duet *This Is Not Real Love,* both lovers recognize their failed romantic loving relationship — without their realising that their relationship has moved to companion love.

Reciprocal exploitation is Mutya's way to avoid being alone in George's absence in a world she does not understand. For George, it is his holding on to her for the comfort she offers, even though he believes she is ready to leave him. Recognizing this exploitation, both think there is no love left, but this is not true as mutual exploitation and exploitation of the relationship as a whole are not the determinant factors of real love. Their relationship remains as emotionally deep and broad as most romantic relationships, and the way they speak to one another and call each other darling reflects this.

Their strong emotional bond assures the lovers' attendance and tending of each other whenever called upon, although they are prepared to accept a romantic relationship with someone else and move on, but they do not realise companion love is there between the lines. However the confusion of this mutually exploitative companionship, where romantic intimacy is now sexual comfort, means it is destined to founder the moment either one finds their greater good elsewhere.

Friendship Love
Friendship love values honesty and equity and rejects exploitation. This is unmistakably similar to romantic love and many people consider that romantic lovers are friendship lovers too, reinforcing the ideal of romantic lovers who are best friends.

In Ricky Martin's song *She's All I Ever Had*, he boasts that the absent beloved was his lover and friend,[119] but close as romantic lovers seem to be to friendship lovers in terms of honesty, equity and the rejection of exploitation, romantic intimacy is solely a romantic love attribute, a secondary condition that prevails the moment you bestow love upon your romantic beloved. In setting this condition, you take abstracted ownership of your romantic beloved as your romantic beloved.

This is different to your bestowal of love upon a friend where such intimacy is explicitly excluded.

Beyond the absence of romantic intimacy in such a friendship, there are two other crucial differences between friendship and romantic love. The first is trust, which revolves around the rejection of jealousy, something not usually found in romantic love. The second is equity, which covers equality and liberty. While both of these are present in romantic love, they embody more the spirit of friendship than romantic love.

No Romantic Intimacy
The most striking difference between romantic and friendship love is the secondary condition of no romantic intimacy in act, attitude or duties. Romantic intimacy is the red line between romantic and friendship love, and all friend love types include this secondary condition.

The 1989 romantic comedy *When Harry Met Sally* and the 2011 romantic drama *Friends with Benefits* both dramatize the challenge faced by lovers on both sides of the no romantic intimacy red line.

The underlying premise in *When Harry Met Sally* is that men and women cannot be friends as sexual attraction gets in the way. Harry tells Sally when they first meet that men and women are incompatible as friends[120], but then struggles to come to terms with his attraction and unplanned friendship with her, while she takes their friendship love for granted since he is not explicitly pursuing her romantically.

Despite this, sexual attraction and romantic jealousy are felt but suppressed by both as their friendship blossoms, until tipping point when they engage in sex[121] and recognize that romantic intimacy is the boundary between friendship love and romantic love, and conclude they are at an impasse.

The drama is the risk of Harry or Sally losing their beloved friend by realizing that this relationship must be romantically intimate.

The film shows that a beloved is either a beloved friend or a beloved romantic lover. Abstracted ownership cannot be of both friend and lover at the same time, because many of the secondary conditions of friendship love are at odds with romantic love when roles and duties are applied.

In *Friends with Benefits,* when Dylan moves to New York he suggests to Jamie that their friendship include sex, which she accepts as long as it is for pleasure only with no romantic love expected.[122]

Both use their relationship to overcome the loneliness of living in a big city and explicitly seek advantage in their careers and financial positions. Since one will leave the other when the time is right, the relationship is of companion love, not friendship love, that supports their no-strings-attached sex for enjoyment.

Nevertheless, the agreement of no romantic love becomes unsustainable as sex becomes romantic intimacy and a catalyst for bringing about a shift from friendship or companionship to romantic love. To achieve transition the lovers must discard their perfect-imperfect friend or companion, and the duties that come with these relationships, and take up abstracted ownership of the perfect-imperfect romantic beloved.

When the lovers' romantic intimacy secondary condition changes to *romantic intimacy must be present*, followed by an equivalent desire to change abstracted ownership to 'romantic beloved', the lovers cross from one love to the other under a new set of conditions and duties.

In both *When Harry Met Sally* and *Friends with Benefits*, the lovers battle successfully with the romantically intimate red line, although many struggle to define the line, let alone cross it, fearing the loss of a close friend. In Luther Vandross' song *If I Didn't Know Better* he tells his beloved friend he is confused about their relationship because she treats him as her romantic lover. Because she stays with him all the time and signals romantic intimacy by touching him, he wonders whether to change their relationship to one of romantic lovers by crossing the red line. He thinks friends have fun and are less physical, unlike romantic lovers who are romantically intimate. His beloved risks their relationship by the things she does.[123]

Friends walk towards the horizon side by side agreeing on no romantic intimacy. Romantic lovers agreeing to physical and emotional romantic intimacy look into one another's eyes with their backs to the world and let life revolve around them. This is primarily why friends and romantic lovers are so different from one another.

Trust and Jealousy

In general, love and jealousy are lovers — and love and trust are friends. Most romantic lovers demand monogamy and suppress the desire for sex with others. Popular media proclaim that sexual affairs are commonplace, but lead to the withdrawal of love, so jealousy is a strong attribute of romantic love.

However, jealousy runs contrary to friendship, because idealized friendship suppresses it. This does not mean friends cannot feel jealousy, but a friend's aim is the betterment of one's friend, which is only achieved when friends accept each other's freedom to befriend others and spend time away as they wish, at the same time avoiding jealousies through an honest, open relationship.

The 2011 movie *Something Borrowed* dramatizes the suppression of jealousy within friendship and brings to light the difference between friendship and companion love. The story revolves around two relationships: the female friends, Rachel and Darcy, and the female and male friendship of Rachel and Ethan. Rachel and Darcy's relationship is depicted as friendship love, although it is really a friendship/companionship, and Rachel and Ethan's relationship is a reciprocal friendship.

Rachel has always given to Darcy, and Darcy takes from Rachel. When Rachel introduces Darcy to her beloved college friend Dex, both women are romantically attracted to him, but Rachel suppresses her attraction and her friend and romantic jealousies as Darcy takes up a romantic relationship with him.[124] As Darcy and Dex distance themselves from Rachel when they fall in love, she feels the loss of two friends and a potential romantic beloved, and abandons her posture of suppression of romantic and friend jealousies.

Rachel and Ethan's relationship demonstrates greater clarity on the suppression of jealousy between friends.

Although Ethan is romantically attracted to Rachel, he tells her to go to Dex, rejecting his romantic desire and denying himself the good he would like to possess — reciprocated romantic love with Rachel — to hold on to the other good he possesses, the perfect-imperfect friendship, proving to himself the active attribute of suppressed jealousy. He does this in pursuit of holding on to the friendship he has with Rachel based on the principle of 'betterment of the beloved'.[125]

Although the relationship between Rachel and Darcy is a friendship/companion love, Luke Greenfield, who wrote the film script, seeks to portray a reciprocal friendship pushed to its limits. The essence of the film is how friends deal with something only one friend can have, in this case one man's love, and by doing so forego the friendship they value.

Rachel is shown as a friend and Darcy as a companion until Rachel switches to companion by abandoning the principles of friendship. This highlights Rachel's suppression of jealousy as expected within friendship love, but she then abandons friendship by acting upon her jealousy as a companion would. Ethan continues to suppress his jealousy within his true reciprocal friendship love with Rachel. Greenfield argues that a friendship/companion loving relationship sinks to the lowest common denominator — mutual companion love — when either lover wants the greater good that the other cannot have. In contrast, the lowest common denominator for true friendship will always be suppression of jealousies based on the betterment of the beloved.

Equity

Like a coin, equity has two faces — equality and liberty — both of which set friendship apart from all other loves, romantic love in particular.

Equality is a shared attitude, where each friend sees the other as equal to themselves, regardless of external factors such as intellect, roles within the wider community, their jobs, their pecking order within family, and their birthright in the broader sense.

Liberty is a shared attitude, where each friend recognizes the freedom of the other in that their relationship is one of independence, not dependence or interdependence. This is in sharp contrast to romantic love. Romantic jealousy is an inhibitor to liberty placed upon the beloved by the lover. In the same context, friend jealousy may also be an inhibitor as jealousies that might threaten the relationship through mistrust surface and yet are suppressed because they restrict liberty, and with them the independence friends value. In *Something Borrowed* Ethan steps back as Rachel's romantic relationship with Dex flourishes, even as he feels his friend slip away, in the knowledge that she is free to come and go, love whom she chooses romantically and as a friend, and their friendship remains strong.

The 2009 movie *The Soloist* highlights attributes of equality and liberty in the relationship between Steve Lopez and Nathanial Ayers as the friendship develops between the two men who are worlds apart in social standing.[126] Steve is a white, American, middle-class columnist for the Los Angeles Times while Nathanial is African American, homeless and a talented musician who suffers from schizophrenia.

Steve tries to equalize Nathanial to create a bond of friendship by pressing him to have his condition treated and taking him away from what he considers a life of depravity on the streets. This impinges on Nathanial's liberty and misinterprets that to be equal means Steve being equal in attitude.

Steve realises friendship includes equality and liberty and that there are things he should not change if Nathanial is to be his friend.[127] The crystallisation of friendship he seeks can only occur if he respects the liberty of Nathanial as an independent, equal beloved who can choose for himself how he sees himself, how he lives, and his treatment.

Romantic lovers are not as liberated or equal as friends, due to their high degree of dependence and interdependence.

In *The Soloist*, friends expect few constraints and neither limits the other in deed or thought. Romantic lovers, on the other hand, place many constraints upon one another as they rely on shared needs, rights and duties. Many of the films with romantic themes cited so far show how dependent and interdependent romantic lovers tend to be and how much pressure beloveds put on their lovers to be as they want and do as they ask.

Pressure to change or act is avoided within friendship as friends pride themselves on their independence. As a result the friendship lover suppresses the urge to impose upon the beloved's sense of equity, and the beloved suppresses deeds they think will impinge upon this sense of equity.

Romantic lovers accept duties and restrictions from their beloved, whereas friends avoid placing such obligations on how their beloved should think or act, and whom they should befriend or bestow romantic love upon out of respect for their liberty and equality. This is because friends seek independence as two equal minds and two equal souls bound by shared values within their community of two. Romantic lovers tend to forego their independence within their community of two as two souls with their backs to the world, bound by love within the liberal romantic ideal.

♥

Given the differences between friendship and romantic love, you would think we would recognize their inconsistency, but many romantic lovers proudly refer to their beloved as both friend and lover, and outsiders admire, even envy, such perfect love.

Before the mid-20th-century, friendship and romantic love were not such good bedfellows, but equity has fundamentally changed attitudes towards romantic love.

Western culture today is infused with equality and liberty, the two elements of equity. And throughout the liberal media, we see a strong message of pride in independence, self-reliance and free-thinking, and a desire to seek for ourselves what we feel we deserve. Such ideas of liberty based on the principles of equality reflect a significant change in society from 70 years ago. Added to this, sexual liberation for women holding on to the romantic ideal shows why romantic love is converging with friendship. Why should the role of female romantic beloved affect the pursuit of independence, self-reliance and freethinking? And why should any man reject this if he wants his beloved to possess the good she seeks in loving him? And, in a broader sense, any beloved regardless of gender?

In the song *You're My Best Friend*, Queen reflects the modern attitude of romantic and friendship love as one loving relationship. They are proud to tell the world how special the friend is, and at the same time how much they love them as a romantic beloved.[128] This means they think love is bestowed in two ways at the same time: one romantically, based on the perfect-imperfect romantic beloved, and the other as a friend based on the perfect-imperfect beloved friend.

Such parallel bestowal must result in accepting several secondary conditions to support the inclusive loves of both roles.

Romantic lovers have specific roles to play with duties that deny them elements of equity they would enjoy as friends — for instance children and the resulting lifestyle changes place restrictions on romantic lovers because of the duties and conferred rights that come with family life.

This is not to say mothers should stay home as dutiful homemakers and fathers take on the breadwinner role in a traditional sense. These outdated roles are breaking down, mostly because of the change in attitude towards equality, but one of the lovers is a mother and the other is a father in a nuclear family sense, and within these roles come differing limitations and obligations on each parent externally and internally. Family role limitations are absent in friendship love, because friends are independently equal and liberal.

Beyond role-based pressures on romantic lovers, jealousy is rarely suppressed in romantic love but heavily suppressed in friendship. For romantic lovers, jealousies include who the beloved befriends and how they interact with others across family, extended family and circles of friends. Friendship lovers suppress such jealousies, and friends are free to take on other non-sexual, sexual and romantically intimate relationships with whomever they wish, usually without the beloved censuring them.

Because friendship and romantic love are so different, the modern liberal romantic view that suggests romantic lovers are also friends is a contradiction in terms, although the protagonist in Queen's song is convinced his romantic beloved is also his friend.

The answer is in the way he wants to present his loving relationship to the world. He aims to show that the love he shares with his beloved has many of the qualities of friendship and seeks to portray the idea of trust over suppressed jealousy, depth and breadth in knowing one another intimately, and equity in both equality and liberty terms, all qualities which are considered admirable in romantic relationships.

His message plays chiefly to women who are equal to men under Western law and in most Western societies. Queen's protagonist is a modern man singing to a modern audience. He merges 20th-century romantic love, social equality and the age-old friendship love attributes of independence, trust and equity, reflecting the ideal of romantic love becoming one with friendship love — something romantic lovers must seek as their good. This is a massive change when you consider brides promised to honour and obey grooms on their wedding day just 30 or 40 years ago.

Many qualities of friendship can be injected into romantic

love — differing degrees of independence, equality and as much liberty as possible. Where qualities of friendship are added, many romantic couples are better off, but the secondary conditions of both types of love, although similar in theory, are different in application. For this reason, friendship and romantic love are mutually exclusive.

Comrade Love

Comrade love tends to happen by chance, when two people find themselves in an unexpected situation that forces them to cooperate towards a specific common good, such as war or abandonment in a harsh environment — a barren desert, aboard a stricken ship, in tundra or up a mountain.

It is present when two lovers, who under other circumstances might not necessarily be friends or companions, find themselves in a situation of interdependence and cooperate to either survive or bring an ideal to fruition against a hostile environment. They form a relationship where they create value in one another through commitment and attachment and, through the three-pillar model, bestow love upon one another. At this point they bestow immense value upon one another, assure commitment to attend and tend, and take up abstracted ownership, so in these terms, comrade love is no different from any other type of love. It need not be reciprocal, although it is most effective when reciprocated.

Comrade love shares many attributes of friendship and companion love, but its distinguishing attributes include interdependence, impermanence, trust, equity and selfish concern.

Interdependence

As two people find themselves facing a common struggle such as oppression, a harsh environment or a call to arms, there comes a time when they realise they share their fate and must make a conscious decision to either cooperate if they are to stand a chance or reject cooperation and lessen the odds by going it alone. Even when only one choice seems viable, the decision to enter into an interdependent relationship is not made under duress or out of duty, but from how to overcome a common struggle. This is the first step towards comrade love. The lover knows that only through shared acts will they achieve the outcome sought beyond the relationship. In the 1958 film *The Defiant Ones*, this is to escape those chasing them, and as convicts on the run the two men are shackled together, so neither can achieve this alone.

Their realization of interdependence begins when Joker and Cullen fight over which direction they should run in. Joker wants to run south and Cullen north, because as an African American Cullen knows he will stand out in the South and be caught, whereas Joker, a white American, prefers not to run north towards a train that may no longer be running.[129] Each man knows they are the means to the other's ends and an underlying sense of value, commitment and attachment operates as they bond during their joint struggle.

Impermanence
Impermanence is a distinctive feature of comrade love. Knowing the relationship will come to an end sooner rather than later brings the comrades together, focused on whatever outcome binds them.

Outside the relationship comrades find themselves in, it may be apparent that they would otherwise be at odds with each other regarding their differing values, so it is only the brief struggle that brings comrade lovers together, not their shared values as found in friendship. Because of this mismatch in values — whether morality, loyalty, servitude or duty to an external world order — comrades understand and accept the temporary nature of their love bestowed.

Joker considers African Americans below White Americans like himself in social status whereas Cullen believes that inequality based on race is improper. Because of the short-lived nature of their relationship and need for interdependence, Cullen must set aside this mismatch in values for the short term. He will do so if Joker suppresses his racism, which Joker must do to achieve his ends.

They agree on a common set of values for the duration of

their comradeship. These values take shape as they agree they were a convicted crook and a murderer and accept it is right and proper to be equal, regardless of race, and of trusted character within their community of two, in the short-term at least.[130]

Friendship and companion lovers share respect for their beloved's needs, rights and values across the board and in the long run.

Trust

Because of the binding interdependence to overcome shared struggle, trust is an active attribute of comrade love. Distrust initially drives a wedge between Joker and Cullen, but in the end an understanding of trust brings them together as comrade lovers. As with all loving relationships, trust is part of the secondary condition set of each lover, but is often offset in the pursuit of the good, which introduces distrust.

Equity

Equality is necessary in loving comradeship, especially where lovers recognize outside values that would otherwise deny equality between them. The community of two creates its own sense of equality within and disregards all inequalities that would otherwise be introduced from outside their community.

In comrade love, its underlying interdependence limits the liberty of each lover within the context of the shared struggle; while independence frees friends to do as they please within the context of goodwill.

The underlying condition of liberty in comradeship is bound to interdependence, equality and trust, but none of these take away from the voluntary nature of comradeship in terms of bestowal, ongoing bestowal and withdrawal of love within or after the shared struggle.

The question is when to end the comradeship by withdrawing love.

This aspect of liberty to choose to enter, stay and leave a comradeship under free will is important as it demonstrates that comrade love is free.

Selfish Concern

Rarely seen in other types of love selfish concern supports the concept that you need not be my friend, nor I yours, but through you I can survive this struggle and so can you through me. In this context, each comrade must see their comrade as necessary to save themselves. Here, you bestow love on similar lines of self-love, but your needs or secondary conditions at the reasoned layer become selfish concern where *I look after you to look after myself. And if you do not meet my needs in looking after me to look after yourself I will not assure you of my commitment to attend and tend.*

By accepting such a mutually exploitative relationship through selfish concern, the other attributes of interdependence, impermanence, trust and equity fall into place. Once in place, the necessary conditions of love are realised: i.e., immense value in the beloved, assured commitment to attend and tend, and abstracted ownership of the perfect-imperfect comrade.

Chapter 14

Social Love

Social love is not the love of an ideal such as a perfect society, nor is it patriotism. Social love is the love of people within a society, expressed either as 'societal love' where the lover loves all those within a given society, or 'human love' where the lover loves all humans by virtue of their humanity within a humanitarian or religious context.

Societal Love

Societal love is close to but broader than the fellowship love seen in religious love. Societal lovers consider society as a host of individuals who live under a single body politic, forming a state with defined culture and institutions. In this context, the bestowal of love upon all people in a society is one-to-many, but unlike fellowship love it does not seek a many-to-one reciprocation.

We may live in social groups because we are social animals by nature and like living close to one another within one body politic, or because our limbic system makes us feel good when we are physically close to others, and uncomfortable in their absence. Maybe birds flocking together give us a benefit we seek. Yalom suggests that existence pain brings us together and eases the inevitability of death, our ultimate aloneness, and the absence of any meaning or sense to life while allowing us to plan our own lives[131] — or we may live in social groups for safety and protection.

At any rate, societies are made up of like-minded individuals from different families and ethnic and regional groups. This is an oversimplification of our diverse cultures and the institutions that govern them, and includes dominating, governing cultures driven by both good and bad motives.

Citizens[XXVI] of any society come from different groups with different religious backgrounds and degrees of wealth and political power. Tensions, frictions and even hatred cause violent protests on significant issues such as war, economic equality, the environment, race relations — expressed in terms of religion or immigration — and social policies.

Some groups stand out from the society their members originally belonged to, and history has shown that families, gangs, regional and political movements, and religious fellowships will fight to the death if necessary for group doctrine over broader societal cultural norms and obligations.

In light of these points, how is it possible to love everyone in a society when individuals, both alone and in groups, violently reject that same society and, along with it, the lover?

And how can the lover love society on a one-to-all basis when some members of it believe themselves unequal to the lover and fellow members? Does the lover consider themself equal to the whole of society, and does the lover need to love everyone?

Are the financially impoverished in a society equal in:

- ♥ Freedom of movement
- ♥ Whom they associate with
- ♥ What they are allowed to say
- ♥ Whether they may vote
- ♥ Access to essential resources such as food, water, warmth and health care
- ♥ Access to advanced resources such as information, justice and family planning.

The same questions arise in terms of differences in race, sex, sexual orientation, education and disability.

Undoubtedly there is inequality within and throughout society and, as the lover, you may find yourself in groups of high

---

[XXVI] Citizen means member of society in general not necessarily a legal or naturalized member of a given society.

or low social status, but within the context of societal love all citizens are loved equally.

Returning to Plato's *scala amoris*, for him societal love is another step on the lover's ascension to the afterlife.[132] To achieve societal love, he says, there must be a realization by the lover that all people in the society are beautiful. What he means is that the lover must see them as perfection in body and soul, so as to bestow love upon everyone as beautiful individuals in their own right and yet as one and the same.

Plato creates this one and the same beauty, where no forms are ugly on a person-to-person level. Such forms reduce love objects — in this case individuals — to one set of quintessential attributes.[133]

He creates his citizen form or perfect or beautiful love object by stripping people of every attribute that differentiates them such as lover, hater, healthy, diseased, rich, poor, aesthetically appealing or unappealing, intelligent or unintelligent and so on. Only what is shared by everyone is left, so metaphorically everyone becomes a number, the same number. When Plato applies this form of citizen to all citizens and then bestows his love upon all as equally perfect — actually equally pure — you become perfect because you are quintessentially a beautiful citizen. And I love you regardless of any difference there may be, and whether you reject me.

Applying a platonic form and loving it in this way is overly simplistic as forms such as these strip people of the individual vibrancy that enables a culture of passionate individuals. Since societal love is the love of all within a given society, I believe it is more than the citizen form can represent.

An identity mosaic, the veil of assent and the Stradivarius effect serve societal love better than forms. As a societal lover, you can create a single identity mosaic of a typical citizen by collecting descriptors of everything you know about people within your society and applying them in order of importance, filtering out the irrelevant ones by pushing them beyond the veil. You apply the Stradivarius effect on what remains within the veil to create the perfect-imperfect typical citizen — a perfect-imperfect love object that is each and every member of society, but also includes the vibrancy of society, regardless of each individual's attitude.

This is not to say platonic forms that strip all citizens down to their most basic attributes are useless for societal love. You may prefer to adopt this approach to create your perfect beloved, but the typical citizen created through the veil and Stradivarius effect creates vibrancy and captures the essence of humanity. Loving sentiment then plays a more significant part for the lover, who seeks and embraces connections with individuals within their society. This supports immense value based on the emotional sentiment that accompanies assured commitment to attend and tend and abstracted ownership more than the cold rational logic of forms.

Fearless on the Pink Floyd album *Meddle* demonstrates the difference between the two approaches, where at the end you hear a capacity crowd of Liverpool football fans singing *You'll Never Walk Alone*. Coming from the British city of Liverpool and having stood in Anfield Football Stadium during a game, the richness of a crowd in spontaneous harmony is within my British citizen veil and high in importance.[134] Platonic forms would strip this attribute of people spontaneously singing since not everybody can sing, nor wants to sing, but by using the veil of assent and Stradivarius effect the lover embraces these descriptors.

For any lover to bestow love upon all individuals in a given society, either through the platonic form or the veil, they must accept several secondary conditions, the first being: *my bestowal of love upon all individuals within this society need not be reciprocated by all other members*. This condition sets societal and fellowship love apart. The fellowship's refusal to reciprocate the lover's bestowal prevents the lover from becoming a legitimate member of the fellowship. This brings about infatuated or delusional love, although in societal love no expectation exists as the lover may be a citizen regardless.

Another secondary condition the lover must accept is: *my bestowal upon all within this society is regardless of the rejection of my bestowal by some members*. This condition recognizes that each individual is free to reject your love, although their refusal is not a condition of your bestowal — you are not entering into an 'in love' relationship as seen in romantic love where reciprocation is necessary for a bond to be crystallized. Your love, including abstracted ownership, may remain intact provided you wish to maintain it.

You need not bestow love upon every individual in society. You can exclude some by pushing them out of your veil or not recognizing them in your form. The typical citizen beloved, representative of everything inside your veil, does not share these traits on the grounds you do not consider them relevant to the perfect-imperfect citizen. In fact, by including them inside your veil and applying the Stradivarius effect, the result becomes imperfect, which taints the perfect-imperfect typical citizen to the point of total rejection of societal love. When this happens, it is necessary to exclude some individuals from your veil to support the purity of the beloved who represents the perfect-imperfect typical citizen. Beneath such exclusion lies the dark side of societal love.

The exclusion of individuals linked to their strong traits leads to their devaluation and marginalization.

The same is true of platonic forms where individuals are considered another group or set. Those without Greek citizenship would have had a form of their own, excluding them from Plato's bestowal of love. In modern terms, long resident but unnaturalized immigrants may be and often are excluded from the citizen form or typical citizen by anyone seeking to marginalize them.

Human Love

Human love is like societal love in that the lover bestows love on a one-to-many basis and does not seek many-to-one reciprocation, but bestowal is upon all humans without distinction of social group. The lover bestows without any distinction as the virtue of being human is enough for love, although the lover's grounds for bestowal come from one of two doctrines: religious doctrine or humanitarianism.

Christian charity is defined by the Vatican as "...*the theological virtue by which we love God above all things for his own sake, and our neighbour as ourselves for the love of God."*[135] Charity combines love with loving God and the love of others as if they were ourselves. Where the lover chooses to love all humans like this, each individual is considered one and the same by virtue of God's creation and their being an analogue of the lover.

Humanitarian love is not entangled with religious belief. The lover bestows by virtue of each beloved's humanity on humanitarian[XXVII] grounds. The mechanism for this love can be through platonic forms to create the form 'human' or the veil of assent and Stradivarius effect to create the perfect-imperfect 'typical human'.

As in societal love, there may be exclusions where the lover chooses to reject individuals or groups from the human form or typical human, usually done to demonize and marginalize groups of people on ethnic, religious or other grounds for political purposes.

As our ability to create life and develop artificial intelligence increases, the question of what is human and what is not will also be challenged. In the 1999 movie *Bicentennial Man,* Andrew, an android with human traits, petitions humanity to recognise him as human because without recognition he is not loved by humans or treated like a human.[136]

[XXVII] Referring to humanitarianism as an informal doctrine whereby people take on a duty is to support and promote human welfare based on the principle of bettering humanity for moral, altruistic and logical reasons.

Part 4
Inanimate Love

Love is a fabric woven by nature and embroidered by imagination.

—VOLTAIRE[137]

Chapter 15

Things Real and Imagined

The inanimate loves include object and ideal love, which expose the complex way in which the human mind operates in a dimension of ideas and imagination and how we interact in the real world.

Chapter 16

Love of Things

We either love an object in relation to our identity, 'identity object love', or to our participation in the world, 'experience object love'. The difference between the two is our attitude towards the object loved. Where we elevate an object to a role such as a friend, a pet, a pursuit or even a romantic beloved, it falls into object love as we merge the beloved into our identity to express our self-identity or to extend self in pursuit of a greater good.

In contrast, for experience object love we absorb moments of experience and bestow love upon them so as to love current immersive experiences, or a collection of memories of past immersive experiences, or even predictive thoughts of experiences for an imagined future. These can, and often do, form part of the lover's identity within object love.

Identity Object Love
'*No man is an island,*' wrote the 16th-century poet, John Donne, '*Every man is a piece of the continent, a part of the main*', meaning that we should view ourselves as an inevitable part of humanity, yet inasmuch as we are integral to humanity, we also value self and seek recognition as individuals.

One way we create individuality while remaining part of the main is by defining self through our things: clothes, jewellery, cars, houses, collectables, and the money, investments and insurances that protect these things and us. Such defining things can also be a way of life, a career or a persona, and these tangible and intangible objects create 'a view of self', 'an expression of self', or 'an extension of self', so that beloved objects become a defining part of self.XXVIII

Lover's View of Self
Your mind holds a single mosaic of self that includes:

- ♥ Self-assessment of your physical and psychological self with applied importance and clustering
- ♥ Memories of what you have done and thought
- ♥ Descriptors of other people's identity mosaics of you based on what they have seen and heard about you, but qualified with importance and clustering
- ♥ All abstracted objects you have tagged with legitimate ownership, as regards your bestowal of love upon them.

This comprehensive view of self gives you a sense of reality and shapes the way you feel about yourself and the people around you. By explaining what you are and guiding you towards what you think you should be, it also offers you insight into your essence. All of this is within the context of Sartre's theory that our existence precedes our essence. You are born and then take on identity by the things you choose to do, including what you claim is yours and attach to your self-identity.

In *For Love of the Game* (1999), Billy has spent his whole life trying to play perfect baseball. The film compares him as a baseball player to his experiences as a romantic lover with his beloved Jane, when he strays from the pursuit of perfection.

After an injury, Billy accuses Jane of holding him back and asks if she has ever loved anything as much as he loves baseball. His self-identity is anchored to his love of the game as it is integral to how he sees himself.[138]

Jane leaves him, concluding he loves baseball not her, but

XXVIII These three kinds of love (view of self, expression of self, extension of self) have been extrapolated from the paper '*I Love It! – Towards a unifying theory of love across diverse love objects*' by Aaron Ahuvia (1993) available from Source: http://deepblue.lib.umich.edu/bitstream/handle/2027.42/35351/b169831x.0001.001.pdf?sequence=2&isAllowed=y

she is wrong. He loves them both. The critical distinction is that the game as a love object is so integrated with whom he sees himself to be that he would lose his sense of self without it, whereas Jane is independent of his sense of self. Therefore, his desperation to return to health and pursue perfection once more in baseball is a reflection of his fight to hold on to his essence: a baseball player.

When we perceive objects as self-defining, we love them on the condition they remain integral to our self-identity. Otherwise we seek other objects that do that, leaving the original beloved behind by withdrawing our love or loving them on new terms.

Lover's Expression of Self

In contrast to the love of objects that the lover considers integral to self-identity, lovers may use love objects to express their identity. This love is beyond merely owning objects that portray a persona; instead the lover bestows love upon objects integral to the identity they wish to present to others. Designers, musicians, dancers, writers, poets, sculptors or painters love what they produce because these things portray the lover. In the documentary *van Gogh: Painted with Words*, Alan Yentob explains van Gogh's work and reasoning as he summarizes his hundreds of letters to his brother, Theo. Yentob concludes that van Gogh poured his feelings onto canvas,[139] reflecting a love of painting that gave him the good he sought in creation and also in expressing himself through his art. For example: *"If I succeed in putting some warmth and love into the work, then it will find friends,"* wrote van Gogh to Theo.[140]

As painters, he and Jean-François Millet said that in art one must give one's heart and soul,[141] paraphrasing the Bible's *"And thou shalt love the Lord thy God with all thy heart, and with all thy soul..."*[142] both referring to their love of what they created in the way a Christian loves God, emotionally and spiritually.

Van Gogh's life, which he expressed through *The Potato Eaters*[XXIX] and his other paintings, was a constant battle of self-

---

[XXIX] An online image of Van Gough's *The Potato Eaters* can be found at http://www.wikipedia.com keyword: The Potato Eaters.

expression reflecting his own morality, because he wanted people not to admire, nor approve, but to understand.

Artists such as Millet and van Gogh love their creations because they express who they are physically, emotionally and morally.[143] This draws a distinction between the love of an ideal — the artist's working life which they may or may not see as an ideal — and love of the objects created which was essential to van Gogh as objects defining him.

One of the secondary conditions of the bestowal of love upon an object as an expression of self is that *provided you are an expression of me as the good I seek I will maintain my bestowal of love upon you*. Failing this, where the object is no longer capable of expressing self, or has served its purpose, or where self-expression is no longer sought or the lover is no longer able to exploit the love object, the lover will withdraw their love from the beloved object to bestow upon the next object that serves the lover's purpose.

Lover's Extension of Self
Many objects we interact with every day enable us to achieve things we cannot do alone. A ladder allows us to reach places we otherwise could not; spectacles permit us to see clearly; a car conveys us at our convenience. These things are useful, but not necessarily loved if they merely support access, sight or travel. However objects we highly value for extending ourselves are often loved.

In the 1983 film *Educating Rita*, Rita, a barely educated young woman, bestows love upon education to escape the social trap she is in.

She tells Denny, her husband, that she loves education and learning, but Denny asks her to give it all up to hold their marriage together. He wants children and for her to settle into a life of domesticity with him. Rita refuses sadly,[144] having wept when he burnt her books after discovering she was taking contraceptives, as she now realises that he devalues the good she seeks in loving education: herself in a world free from female domesticity and a future without financial hardship, and thus devaluing the love object itself.

Her love of education is founded on the belief that education would enable her to live a life of good that she would never achieve without it.

Educating Rita illustrates an important aspect of loving objects as an extension of self, but comes with a warning: Rita loves education as the means to an end, self-fulfilment, but once she achieves that end the three-pillar model will fail since her love of education as an extension of self will drop away. This is because the love object loses its value once the lover achieves their good. In Rita's case, once educated she feels self-fulfilled, but the old Yiddish curse tells us to be careful what we wish for as we might just get it, as Rita's friend Trish discovers.[145] The education that Rita loves as an enabler of the good does not give her the good at all.

On this basis, a secondary condition for objects that are an extension of self is: *I'll bestow and maintain my bestowal of love upon this object while it remains the only way to achieve the good I seek.*

Experience Object Love

Loving sentiment plays a vital role in most loving relationships as it shows the lover how they feel about their beloved. In romantic love, loving sentiment includes the three elements of sentiment past, present and future. With these in mind, the lover creates precious memories and thoughts of the good they have enjoyed with their beloved, including everything they know of their beloved in depth and breadth of psyche, the good the lover feels when with their beloved, and the future good the lover predicts.

Current moments and past memories are loved, as are memories of wishful thoughts. A fragmented recollection endowed with nostalgia of a date 30 years ago or a lover's dream of a future wedding can be bestowed with the lover's love. The lover values these memories immensely, and takes abstracted ownership of them while assuring themself they will attend and tend to the memories by holding on to them and retelling them to keep them alive.

Memories created within these elements of past and future are loved objects, even though they are intangible thoughts.

Furthermore, moments may be loved as they happen when the lover is inclined to bestow love.

Some loved memories stand alone in the mind, while others take on significance with real objects. The lover loves a photograph of a past beloved who is no longer accessible, when it is attached to beloved memories. Alone, the photo holds minimal significance, but with loved memories it takes on immense value.

Present Experience Love

Sometimes we are so immersed and in awe within an experience that we bestow love upon it as it happens. This is called present experience love and is a state of grace or love affair. These intense feelings alone are the adjective of love, and the lover's intensity of feelings at a particular moment during the experience creates the desire for present experience love, when the lover will bestow their love for as long as it lasts. In 1986, President Reagan spoke of the seven Challenger disaster astronauts as having *slipped the surly bonds of earth to touch the face of God.* This is transcendental, but sometimes in our existential life there may be a state of grace or love affair.[146]

The 1987 film *Babette's Feast* is the story of Babette, who works as a volunteer cook for a devout sect of Christians in a small hamlet in Denmark. When she wins some money, she decides to lay on an elaborate feast for the community members who reject worldly excess.[147]

The movie has two subtexts:

1. Because of her cooking skills, she can create a love affair for the diners who attend her feast
2. Her love affair with cooking as a professional.

During the feast, the diners come to realise what the food is doing to them. General Lorens Löwenhielm makes a speech with religious overtones that describes the love affair created by the feast that immerses them all, creating a unique moment for reconciliation and the rekindling of romantic relationships.[148] This is only achievable through the act of loving.

When the diners have left, Babette speaks of the love affair she created for herself as an artist by cooking a perfect feast.[149] Her two objectives were the experience she immersed herself in and her love of that experience, which is present experience love.

It is usual for artists to combine these two interests and recognize the good as they create and their love of the creative experience. Many lovers are driven to create by their love of creating. Something similar happens to thrill seekers, but they produce nothing for an external consumer. Thrill seekers immerse themselves in a dangerous experience because they love this short-lived experience of immersion.

Love of the experience from inside the experience marks this type of love.

Past Experience Love

Two aspects of past experience can be loved:

1. Memories of the past the lover considers a historical narrative, including physical keepsakes
2. An object or group of objects the lover considers a proxy for an absent beloved that ties them to past experience.

The lover holds memories in historical narrative as a collection of events, and wraps them up as a narrative to create a love object upon which they bestow love. In the 1942 film, *Casablanca*, past experience love is clear. Rick is an American living in the unoccupied city of Casablanca during World War Two. He once had a loving relationship with Ilsa Lund in Paris, who unbeknown to him was married to a prisoner of war. When Paris falls, she leaves without an explanation. She arrives suddenly at Rick's Casablanca bar with her escaping husband, which revives memories of Paris.[150]

Michael Curtiz, the director, uses both the words and riff of *As Time Goes By* throughout the movie as an anchor to the historical narrative of Paris when the couple were in love. He divides the love story into the run-up to Ilsa's arrival in

Casablanca, Rick's bitterness at her abandoning him and his reaffirmation of his love.

When he discovers she did not reject him, but was torn away by an external force, Rick's love of their historical narrative keeps his love of Ilsa alive.

Using music to tell the audience of loved past experience the way Curtiz does so well is standard for filmmakers.

♥

Lovers may hold on to a physical object and bestow love upon it for its historical context — an essential aspect of past experience love. In *The Sorrows of Young Werther*, Goethe writes that Lotte gives Werther a pink ribbon she often wore and had worn the first day they met. He kissed it "*a thousand times, and in every breath inhaled the remembrance of those happy and irrevocable days*" Werther sees a direct link between the ribbon, his beloved Lotte, and their happy times together.[151]

He writes his loved memories to his friend Wilhelm:

> '*Such, Wilhelm, is our fate. I do not murmur at it: the flowers of life are but visionary. How many pass away, and leave no trace behind — how few yield any fruit — and the fruit itself, how rarely does it ripen! And yet there are flowers enough! and is it not strange, my friend, that we should suffer the little that does really ripen, to rot, decay, and perish unenjoyed? Farewell! This is a glorious summer. I often climb into the trees in Charlotte's orchard, and shake down the pears that hang on the highest branches. She stands below, and catches them as they fall.*'

But Werther knows time is fleeting and fears Lotte will not reciprocate his love.

The ribbon is an intimate reminder of her while she is physically absent but still accessible as a set of loved memories, while also offering him hope that he and Lotte may soon be reunited.

However, Werther's increasing sense of inaccessibility to

Lotte attaches a sense of sorrow to the ribbon. Because love includes an expected good life, loving an object connected to the beloved can be bittersweet as it connects the lover to the beloved historically, which included the good, and at the same time reminds them of their absence, which lacks the good. When Werther finally realises Lotte will not leave Albert, despair leads to thoughts of suicide. He writes to Wilhelm and Lotte:

> 'How warmly have I been attached to you, Charlotte! Since the first hour I saw you, how impossible have I found it to leave you…
> This ribbon must be buried with me: it was a present from you on my birthday. How confused it all appears! Little did I then think that I should journey this road. But peace! I pray you, peace!'[152]

His only tangible relic is the ribbon, an object he loves as it is so entwined with loved memories of the past and an imagined inaccessible future with his beloved Lotte. In despair, Werther shoots himself becoming a martyr to love and to everlasting fame.

♥

One rare type of past experience love is where the lover bestows love upon a proxy object to hold on to the past as in the 1960 film *Psycho*.

Norman Bates suffers from schizophrenic episodes. He loves his dead mother, and notably her corpse, when he is Norman and is overprotective to the point of murder when he is his mother.[153] As the film unfolds, it becomes clear that by holding on to his mother's corpse, Norman is holding on to the past. Whenever things may change, when Norman may form a relationship with a woman, he, as his mother, kills in the same way he killed his mother's lover when she brought a third party into their lives. Norman's innate love of the past and fear of the future manifest themselves in his love of his mother's corpse.

Psycho offers the opportunity to delve into the deluded mind of a lover who accepts their beloved object as a proxy for an absent beloved who anchors them in the past, because they seek to hold on to loved past experiences when the past holds the good, whereas the present and the future do not.

Future Experience Love
The love of future experience is an imagined experience loved. This predictive experience wrapped in a memory is not idealized and so the future experience predicted and loved is pragmatic and wholly achievable by the lover, showing that future experience love is not the love of an ideal.

Billy Elliot (2000) tells the story of an 11-year-old boy raised in working class Northeast England, who takes up ballet. Within his patriarchal culture boys do not do this, but Billy, faced with resistance by his family, pursues dance out of love.

When Billy auditions with The Royal Ballet School, he describes how he feels when dancing. His sentiment is reflective, and yet profoundly projective: dancing takes him beyond the normal. It is invigorating and electrifying and on reflection he loves it as a future experience.[154]

There is no barrier to loving a future experience. You memorise it as a predictive memory, bestow love upon the memory based on its immense value to you, attend and tend to it through your repeated recollection of consciousness and all it represents, and take up abstracted ownership of it as a thought. You do these things to possess the good as you do with any type of love because the beloved, in this case a predictive experience, is perfect-imperfect.

The value pillar is of paramount importance in terms of a continued belief that the projected experience will be good. Where the good of the projected experience is maintained, you will maintain your bestowal of immense value, and with it love. Should the time come when you believe the good no longer exists, you will withdraw your immense value. This is because the future experience no longer satisfies your good. In other words, if Billy finds no good in dancing, he will find the idea of dancing, and the recollected imagined future experience of dancing, to be unworthy of his love.

Chapter 17

Love of Perfection

Ideals are ideas of perfection. They may be very personal ideas of perfection, but in many cases they span society and societies. They are not of the physical world insomuch as they are ideas born of imagination that transcends existence, although ideals may be tied to the physical world and specific objects.

Ideals come about over two steps — first determining the form of the love object, followed by appending particular attributes to create the perfect love object.

If you draw a triangle in the sand, then another and another until the beach is full of triangles, you will discover each one is different from all the others: some will be large and others small; some will be right-angled and others equilateral; some will have thick lines, others thin — they will all vary. This is just one beach of an infinite number of beaches you could fill with theoretically unique triangles, and yet they are all, well, triangles.

Plato concluded that if all objects in a set, such as triangles, are different from one another and yet all the same, there must be a 'form' — an essence or quintessential-ness — that is the purest triangle from which all triangles are derived. This form is the universal triangle, stripped of all the differences that separate other triangles. Plato believed there are forms for all things, and each one is the parent of its children — all derive from the master form. Forms cover everything, from objects and people to ideas. Personness is the form of people stripped of the elements that make them different from one another. Human aesthetic beautyness is the form of human beauty. And loveness is the form of love.[155]

To Plato, each form is the 'perfect' of its children when

compared with all other objects within its set, and the form triangleness is the perfect triangle. But there can be confusion between what is perfect and what is pure: pure is an object stripped of its impurities, which is not necessarily perfect. In fact, a form is pure in that it is the bare essence of all objects within the set it is drawn from, whereas perfection as an ideal is a subjective matter — something for the lover to decide, not a universal constant. To Plato, the perfect wife may be the form, which is also pure, but his form of a perfect wife lacks the additional attributes of perfection that make my wife special to me. So the second step of creating an ideal of perfection is to add to the pure form.

To use the triangle analogy, were Leonardo da Vinci to paint the perfect triangle he would take the form triangleness and add attributes of perfection.

Ideals may be considered an imaginary process, where love objects are created in the mind so as to bestow love upon what we imagine. Or we may discover a painting by Leonardo da Vinci and believe he has painted perfection by taking the form of beautyness and adding the attributes of beauty. By doing this, we may bestow love upon the Mona Lisa as an analogue of beauty in reality, assuming we consider the image a picture of beauty.

Within this context, there are two kinds of love ideals: idealized objects and idealized lifestyles.

Idealized Objects

In loving idealized objects, animate or inanimate, there are transcendental and existential ideals. In the former, the lover loves an object that is not real; in the latter it is real, but becomes imaginatively idealized.

Transcendental Ideals

In transcendental ideals, the lover rejects parts of the imperfect real world and puts their energy into loving idealized objects of perfection beyond it, bestowing love upon imagined idealized beloveds and rejecting potential beloveds. In Woody Allen's 1985 film *The Purple Rose of Cairo*, Cecilia, unhappy and impoverished during the American depression, loves fictional objects including movie characters. Within her ideal, one of her beloveds is rich and handsome with a lifestyle to match and, in her off-screen imagination, he loves her. She visits her local cinema frequently, and one day Tom Baxter, her ideal beloved, walks out of the silver screen and asks her to love him.[156]

By dramatizing the ideals that many people love to escape to through stories, the film contrasts them with the reality of imperfection that they return to as they leave the cinema, turn off the TV or close the book. But this idealism is more than escapism, particularly in immersive media such as film — not only is the idealism of the situations portrayed, but also the concept of platonic forms and our dressing them in attributes of perfection. Allen's parody shows the blurring of what is real and what is not — after all, many celebrities written up in glossy magazines such as *Cosmopolitan*, *Vogue*, *GQ* and *Men's Journal* have all the attributes of the perfect beloved. Through skilful editing and digital photo manipulation of aesthetic imperfections, they are brought into the ideal and it is easy for a consumer who desperately wants to believe to idealize the imperfect into perfection and bestow their love. The entire line between fiction and non-fiction is becoming so blurred today that many people find it difficult to know what is real any more.

The films discussed in this book illustrate how easy it is to blur between imperfect reality and perfect idealism. Luhrmann's *Romeo and Juliet*, Ward's *What Dreams May Come* and Cameron's *Titanic* all include perfect beloveds who are not real, yet these characters are idiosyncratic and show love, sorrow, anger, passion and jealousy. But none have ever lived, nor will they ever live, even though we cry, laugh, blush and feel anxious with them.

In the brothel sequence in *The Purple Rose of Cairo*, Tom rejects the offer of sex with prostitutes because of his love for Cecilia. Emma immediately asks if there are any more men like Tom around.[157] On the surface her question is comedic since the scene portrays the North American moral perfect, Tom Baxter, conversing with the North American amoral perfect, the sex worker — it is like God and Satan comparing notes. But she is also asking what everyone seeking love wants to know: where is my perfect? Or rather, where is my perfect who is just like you? Love is about possession of the good, and Tom is the good who will unlock the good life — and Tom is real, an image performing in the real world.

For Cecilia as an analogue of us, bestowing love upon transcendental objects as analogues of people is easy enough to do, and if she can do it so can we. We see this in teenagers when they say they love a beautiful celebrity and we dismiss it as infatuation and not real, even though to them it is real. The basis of this love is fake perfection as presented in the polished media accompanied by polished editorials in glossy magazines, and we expect them to realize the gap between fact and fiction and forget their infatuation when a real perfect-imperfect beloved appears.

As with all loves, transcendental object idealized love is bestowed with secondary conditions. Cecilia knows Tom is fictional, so where she bestows love her first secondary condition is: *you are imaginary, and I accept that the limitations of your interaction with my outer world are part of my loving you.* This essential secondary condition recognizes love's bestowal upon an abstract object, not a real thing or person. Anything less would result in delusion, where Cecilia would fail to convince herself that Tom is real. This is not possible because, as Sartre says, a healthy mind cannot hide the truth behind a lie.[158]

Another secondary condition would be: *I reject all alternates of your perfection, because my love is based on your unique perfection.* This condition will emerge without this implicit statement in mind, because to own the perfect negates the ownership of all other perfects, including real perfect-imperfects created using the veil of assent and Stradivarius effect. If love is the possession of the perfect, which you already possess, then the pursuit of another perfect, or perfect-imperfect is invalid.

The lover will only reappraise the beloved when confronted with the decision to abandon them, based on the failure of the first secondary condition and limited by the imagined perfect.

These two secondary conditions offer a baseline for love's

bestowal on transcendental object ideals,[xxx] so that if the lover bestows love upon idealized objects and not people, reciprocation is not expected and no secondary condition is needed to reflect this. For romantic ideals however, an added secondary condition is required to satisfy the ideal of romantic love: *you love me regardless of my bestowal of love upon you*. For Cecilia, this condition is critical, because without Tom's bestowal of love upon her in the first place she would never be able to enter a state of reciprocated romantic in love and unlock the good of love she seeks.

It may seem odd that an imaginary beloved should bestow love in any meaningful way upon the lover, but since the beloved is the perfect romantic beloved, and all romantic beloveds reciprocate as a means to support the state of in love, the perfect romantic beloved must include the bestowal of love upon the lover. When Tom says he loves Cecilia, this is what he is reflecting, because as the ideal beloved he removes the potential of delusional romantic in love from Cecilia's mind, which plays to her ideal of perfect love.

To the rational mind, the bestowal of love upon an imagined ideal is delusional, and creating the conditions in the mind to avoid delusion may seem paradoxical, but the abstracted ownership of objects from the real world, such as a real romantic beloved, and bestowal of love by means of such abstraction, regardless of the reality of the beloved, are not delusional to the lover any more than bestowing love upon a cherished memory of a dead and equally abstracted beloved. Imagination and belief in the validity of the imagined in the lover's mind play a considerable role in ideal love, as in all other loves.

Existential Ideals

In contrast to transcendental ideals that include objects of perfection beyond existence, you can elevate to perfection real objects and bestow love upon them, although at this point the

---

[xxx] The platonic love types where reciprocation is needed to create a healthy, loving relationship with the beloved are companion, friendship and comrade love.

idea of platonic forms dressed to perfection becomes a little more complicated.

A form is purely notional. It does not exist in reality because it is information that defines the quintessential attributes of all objects within a set. No matter how many triangles you draw on a beach, every one of them is flawed, as every triangle has at least one attribute above the quintessential attributes of the form (three straight lines, connected end-to-end). Every triangle is unique or specific. It is this specificity beyond the form that brings the object into reality and at the same time prevents the form from entering reality. Consequently, the form triangleness is not a triangle at all, but a collection of attributes, which is a distilled identity that is pure, and similar to an identity mosaic.

Lovers latch onto this specificity when taking real objects and idealizing them against forms. In the lover's mind, the beloved becomes a form of specificity that no objects in a set can match, yet in an idealized way all objects aspire to be. The beloved has no imperfections, unlike all others in the set, only attributes of the form and specificity. The beloved's specificity makes them the idealized perfection they are so that the lover attaches to them only, therefore in this sense my house is not platonically pure, but it is specifically perfect when it has unique attributes applied.

Even the idealizing lover knows nothing is perfect and that they must use the veil of assent and Stradivarius effect to idealize to perfection what would otherwise be the perfect-imperfect beloved.

The beloved is idealized when the lover brings into their veil all attributes they believe to be of the form, and attributes they consider unique of the beloved, even where uniqueness is otherwise platonically imperfect. They leave outside all attributes they believe are not of the form and any specificity — the uniqueness of others — that spans all other objects in the set. Now the veil is populated, the lover applies the Stradivarius effect and the beloved takes on perfection.

The *Mona Lisa* and Fabergé's Easter eggs are idealized by their lovers, who consider them perfect. Their provenance makes them unique, if this is what the idealizing lovers consider the defining attribute of the love objects. Lovers bring such specific provenance for each object into their veil and, by treating their beloved objects in this way, they turn what for others is just a painting or a jewelled ornament from a real state of imperfect into a real state of perfection.

It does not matter to the lovers if the *Mona Lisa's* is fading or the enamel of the egg is not perfect, or what da Vinci or Fabergé were like. These attributes are irrelevant to the perfection of the objects. The unique provenance is what counts as the identity description, which brings about the perfection the beloved idealizes. The lovers see nothing but form and uniqueness smoothed by the Stradivarius effect, and bestow their love upon each object in this context.

However, idealizing people to perfection using forms, specificity, the veil of assent and the Stradivarius effect becomes problematic. In Christina Perri's song *Human*, she desperately wants to be her lover's idealized perfect beloved as this seems to be a condition of bestowal, but each time she tries to act consistently with her lover's preconceived ideal of the form with uniqueness applied she fails, because she is active in existence and an object is passive. Whatever Christina does is under constant appraisal against her lover's ideal as the lover asks how to keep the things she has just done outside the veil.

She fails to be her lover's idealized perfect, for only something that says nothing and is alert and good at all times in a mechanical way can become the perfect idealized object of her lover. She can only ever be a perfect-imperfect human.[159]

The three necessary conditions of love are achievable for the love of existential idealized inanimate objects considering their unchanging nature, yet for people and animate objects the ability of the beloved to keep up with their original perfection or become perfect is challenging, especially where the lover's view of uniqueness is uncompromising.

In the 2010 movie *Black Swan*,[160] Nina, a ballet dancer, is offered the role of Swan Queen in a Bolshoi version of *Swan Lake*. A princess is turned into a swan by a sorcerer and the spell can be broken only by a lover's vow of everlasting love, which would allow her to return to her former self, the beautiful

Princess Odette and, as with all fairy tales, live the good life with the good beloved. Her evil twin, Black Swan, prevents Prince Siegfried, Odette's beloved, from bestowing his everlasting love upon her and Odette kills herself.

The idealized state of perfection Nina seeks and loves is only achieved when she loses herself to the Black Swan alter ego. Thomas, who produces the ballet, tells her that Black Swan is the perfection she seeks and that transcendentally and through herself she will be perfect if she lets herself become the Black Swan. However self-perfection is an impossible state. Only perfect-imperfection is possible, but as a performing artist in pursuit of perfection and self-love this is not what Nina seeks.

The problem with idealization of self and the paradox the lover must come to terms with if they are to love in this way is form and uniqueness in a changing world. Therefore the main secondary condition to expect with this type of love is: *the perfection I imagine the beloved to be is true, even though I know this is beyond what is possible within a changing reality.*

This condition offers the lover a means to bestow love upon the idealized perfect, while at the same time resolving the dichotomy of knowing the underlying truth of imperfection within reality. The problem is that the healthy mind cannot lie to itself. Heyman, Heinz and McLaughlin, who wrote *Black Swan*, portray Nina with psychotic episodes so that she accepts her transformation to the perfect self because she is denied access to Black Swan's alter ego manifesting in Nina's mind both on and off stage. This gives Nina the impression of perfection in reality as she transforms towards the ideal as if she senses and embraces her progression through Black Swan's presence, but cannot explain it.

For the healthy mind, lying to oneself is not rational, and so idealizing self to perfection in *Black Swan* is beyond the norm.

Idealised Lifestyles

Just as there are idealized objects, there are idealized transcendental lifestyles — where the lover loves an ideal way of existence in the afterlife — and existential — where the lover loves an ideal way of existence here on earth — lifestyle ideals.

In both cases there are inner-ideals and outer-ideals.

Transcendental Lifestyles

A transcendental idealized lifestyle is a loved idea of perfection beyond life, which may be part of a larger concept such as immersion in a transcendental outer-ideal of Christian heaven, or something simpler — maybe an immersion into a fantasy afterlife inner-ideal of your wildest dreams. These transcendental ideals differ from the transcendental ideal of the perfect self as an idealized loved object where, as a lover, you do not consider yourself perfect in the afterlife, but end up beyond life in a perfect place regardless of your status.

The film *What Dreams May Come* shows the inner-ideal of a self-constructed afterlife when Chris Neilson dies after a road accident. He finds himself in a place of his own making, [161] not a prefabricated Christian heaven as described in the Bible,[162] but the perfect place and lifestyle which he idealized in life, which he and his wife dreamt of and where they agreed to spend eternity together. His transcendental inner-ideal is just as he and his beloved planned it.[XXXI]

The transcendental inner-ideal lifestyle is 'conditionless' except that *my love of my ideal lifestyle is based on my belief in such an afterlife*. While the lover remains steadfast in their belief in their own dreamt afterlife with its expected good, their bestowed love remains. Therefore, the lover's belief alone within free will is the only self-imposed condition of their love.

The most common outer-ideal in the West is the Christian heaven, where the dead lover ascends to a prefabricated place believed to be perfect. This ideal does not presuppose that the lover or anyone else in heaven will become perfect in the sense of pure and free of original sin, since to be perfect would be equal to God, which Christian doctrine denies. The dead will

---

[XXXI] This is not entirely true as the movie introduces several Christian elements that limit Chris' inner-transcendental lifestyle ideal.

not be perfect, but they may be more pure in death after ascension and sanctification through redemption, but they will still be true to the essence of humanity as fallen souls unless God decides to purge their souls.

Nevertheless, if the lover believes heaven to be perfect, they may adopt it as perfect and consider their lifestyle there as perfect, given the two are mutually inclusive.[XXXII/163] If the lover does not believe heaven to be perfect because of its taint of imperfection, they may use the veil of assent and Stradivarius effect to create a sense of the perfect afterlife based on doctrinal influence, just as lovers of an idealized object do. They bring into their veil descriptors of form and uniqueness and leave outside all other descriptors. Once they apply the Stradivarius effect, they find an idealized view of heaven based on whichever sect's underlying description of heaven they follow.

There are alternatives to a heavenly Christian lifestyle. Some are bound to religious faith and other cults, but the simplest outer-ideal outside religious faith is eternal nothingness, where the lover's psyche — or soul in a spiritual sense — ceases to be. The ideal relies on the belief that the brain, the seat of self, degrades irrecoverably on death so that where there is brain death eternal nothingness prevails. Eternal nothingness leaves an impression of the spirit going somewhere with a lifestyle to lead — like the analogy of yellow being a colour and non-yellow the opposite of yellow, whereas it is the absence of yellow. Where yellow once was, non-yellow is the consequence, so in death, nothingness is the absence of self where non-life is the absence of life. This idealised non-existence, or non-yellow, is perfect in the lover's mind. It is an immensely valuable belief which is attended and tended to within the lover's belief system, and abstractly owned in the same way all loved objects are. The lover rejects all preconceived ideas and ideals of an animated

---

[XXXII] 23:42 "And he said unto Jesus, Lord, remember me when thou comest into thy kingdom / And Jesus said unto him, Verily I say unto thee, Today shalt thou be with me in paradise. Luke 23:42-3. In using the term paradise as a place, and applied to other narratives in the Bible where people are purified when entering heaven, the lover will take up the idea that both the place and the lifestyle are perfect.

afterlife and embraces the ideal of a non-afterlife, a non-existence.

Existential Lifestyles

Unlike idealized transcendental lifestyles, idealized existential lifestyles with narrow-ideals and wide-ideals are perfect ways of living in reality and loved as such.

Love of the narrow-life ideal is not singular. It includes the love of all objects, people and other ideals that together create a lifestyle of total perfection. We see this kind of love when somebody becomes so insular they reject all others, close themselves in and love objects close to them, creating their own community and surrounding themselves with love objects. When a potential romantic beloved enters the lover's life seeking appraisal, the lover's love of the narrow-ideal is brought into question because all objects and people loved by the lover within the narrow-ideal are perfect whereas objects and people from reality are not. Should the lover replace a perfect romantic beloved with an imperfect one, the entire narrow-ideal becomes compromised as the lover's idealized future cannot include known imperfections, even if such imperfection is the perfect-imperfect.

In this situation, lovers seek to make people and objects from the real world perfect to hold on to their loved lifestyle ideal by introducing a secondary condition of their love: *you must be the perfect beloved to be included in my existential narrow-ideal of a perfect lifestyle for me to love you*. This secondary condition puts pressure on the potential beloved to change to meet the perfect sought by the lover or risk withdrawal of their love.

In Citizen Kane, Kane fills the palace and grounds of Xanadu with perfect, precious works of art and keeps Susan his wife in luxurious comfort there, but living surrounded by perfection with her as a narrow-ideal lifestyle fails to satisfy as reality cannot deliver what he desires most from his ideal: perfect love of him.[164]

The secondary conditions surrounding narrow-ideals are an acceptance of the imaginary over reality: *the lifestyle I love is founded upon the imaginary, and I must accept this if I am to hold on to it*.

This condition clarifies the imagined nature of the ideal and all objects and people within it. It also supports the lover's acceptance that they will never be satisfied by their idealized lifestyle. The lover who accepts the condition, takes on the delusional nature of the life they lead and seek to possess. When dramatized lovers of narrow-life ideals die alone and unloved in lavish surroundings, demonstrating the folly of loving an unachievable dream of the perfect life.

♥

Narrow ideals serve only the lover, whereas wide ideals also serve the people around them, regardless of whether they want the good of the lover's ideal. The book *Lost Horizon* is about the wide-ideal lifestyle of Shangri-La. Richard Conway, an anti-war idealist, escapes war-torn Baskul with his brother and several others. Hijackers capture their plane in mid-air and take them to the lamasery of Shangri-La, a lush hidden valley ignorant of war, physical pain, persecution and poverty, deep in the Himalayas.[165]

High Lama Perrault explains that Shangri-La is the wide-ideal lifestyle that will one day replace the present world order.

The book shows the potential of a wide-ideal lifestyle of perfection on earth, but it also reflects a cautionary tale. Those who benefit from such lifestyles are themselves imperfect. People are free, and with freedom comes the choice to stay, leave or break the rules of the perfect lifestyle, potentially ruining perfection.

The lover of the wide-ideal knows this and understands that for their adopted ideal to come to fruition tough decisions lie ahead, and so many lovers see their wide-ideal as a struggle because they must fight whoever resists the ideal's passage into existence. To this end, wide-ideals are usually about the bigger picture of creating the perfect community or state. There is an understanding by the lover that building a social edifice takes sacrifice, time and effort, therefore, the lover loves the perfect end that will inevitably come once they dutifully purge all imperfection from their desired world order.

Several elements must be present for the lover to turn a

wide-ideal lifestyle into reality. Once these are adopted, the lover must bring the ideal's entry further into reality through purge and consolidation. These elements include:

- ♥ The 'word' of the ideal written, spoken and sung that expresses its perfection and the righteousness of those who love it
- ♥ Duties and rights of those who will live within it
- ♥ An association of places and events as a narrative attached to the ideal
- ♥ Physical icons that represent the overarching ideal itself and its history
- ♥ One or many faith-heads
- ♥ Martyrs or symbols of martyrdom, which have sacrificed their lives or liberty for the ideal and, in doing so, have become perfect within the ideal itself.

These elements of wide-ideal lifestyles are found all over the world in religious, social and political movements, because they support the lover's adoption and bestowal of love upon them.

The secondary conditions in bestowing love upon wide-ideal lifestyles are significantly different to those of narrow-ideals, even though both are imaginary. The narrow-ideal secondary condition of *'the lifestyle I love is imaginary, and I must accept this if I'm to hold on to it'* is vastly different to the wide-ideal of *'the lifestyle I love is imaginary, but if I love it now and do all I can to make it real, it will become my reality and remain my beloved for as long as it exists.'*

This is based on a perfect way of life that the lover believes is within reach. When the lover bestows love upon the ideal, they must also bring it into reality. Consequently, lovers of wide-ideals change the way they live not only to align their lives to the ideal, but to endeavour to bring it into reality for everyone. This leads to another secondary condition: *as my love is bestowed upon an ideal that I seek to prove exists, I must reject all objects, people and ideals that threaten the ideal's passage into existence. Once it is in existence, I must reject all objects, people and ideals that threaten its survival if I'm to hold onto the beloved ideal.*

This condition is the ugly side of wide-ideal lifestyles.

For those who impede the ideal's passage into existence and its survival, 'just' conflict follows[XXXIII] and leads to the slogan 'by all means necessary' once the lover bestows love upon the ideal and adopts its duties and righteousness. This secondary condition justified ethnic and religious extremism during the Middle Ages, and destructive social and political ideology in the 20th-century. The human cost of these loved wide-ideals is in the millions as leaders have persuaded zealous followers to accomplish their ideal, annihilating whoever failed to fit the perfection sought[XXXIV].

Such tragedies will repeat themselves until humanity recognizes its remarkable ascent[XXXV]. Humans need not kill others on the grounds of ethnic, social or political idealism. *Every human being is valuable just because they are human.* Knowing that this ideal will never be realized is no reason to abandon it, or even not to work towards it. Martin Luther King Jr said *"Darkness cannot drive out darkness; only light can do that. Hate cannot drive out hate; only love can do that."*[166]

[XXXIII] A reference to *Just War Theory*. Where there is justification for righteous action seeking justice; oppressed and oppressor, who is who in just conflict?

[XXXIV] For the 20th-century alone, human cost is estimated to be ~153 million including those who died in the former USSR gulags and Chines equivalent political prisons, the Russian Civil war, World War II and wars and conflicts post-WWII most of which included an undertow of political, ethnic or religious ideology. Source: *Deaths in Wars and Conflicts in the 20th Century* by Milton Leitenberg: Cornel University, Peace Studies Program Occasional Paper #29 3rd Ed. Aug 2003,2005, 2006 ISSN 1075-4857

[XXXV] Recognition of Dr. J. Bronowski's *The Ascent of Man* documentary series (1973) BBC where he argues social development of mankind is evolutionary, positively progressive, enlightened by science and industry, and in concert with art.

Part 5

Religious Love

All, all for Immortality!
Love, like the light, silently wrapping all!

—WALT WHITMAN[167]

Chapter 18

Love in Faith

Four hundred years before the birth of Jesus Christ, Plato said that love in one of its many forms is how people communicate with the divine.[XXXVI]/[168] This message of love's place in divinity has mutated, for the Christian at least, to the Apostle John claiming that God is love.[169] From this, Christian scripture has expanded and clarified that not only is God love but all He creates — everything — He infuses with love. Furthermore, because of God's infusion, everything must be loved. This includes God's will and His followers, as stated in the doctrine of Christianity.[XXXVII]

These ideas of love differ from the Greek and pagan beliefs, which preceded Christianity, as they form an integrated system bound by love through the Godhead. The system's strength is in its four love types, each tied to God, which are stronger together than separately. These loves, adopted by Christianity and culturally integrated across the West, include Eros, Philia, Agapē and Nomos, all of which directly relate to God as Love and love's bestowal.

[XXXVI] Socrates' Speech on Diotema's teaching of love's essence is in Plato's *Symposium*. "He [Love] is a great spirit (daimon), and like all spirits he is the intermediate between the divine and the mortal…" "…He interprets between gods and men, conveying and taking across to the gods the prayers and sacrifices of men, and to men the commands and replies of the gods; he is the mediator who spans the chasm which divides them, and therefore in him all is bound together, and through him the arts of the prophet and the priest, their sacrifices and mysteries and charms, and all prophecy and incantation, find their way."

[XXXVII] Part five is focused on the characteristics of Christian love alone.

Chapter 19

Eros

Eros as an aspiring love, is the bestowal of love by the Christian on a destination which all Christians seek to enter,[XXXVIII/170] the Kingdom of Heaven.

The word eros brings romantic love to mind more than an aspiring love towards heaven because of Cupid, the Roman equivalent of the Greek god Eros, the mischievous god of desire who shoots his arrows of love haphazardly at the madding crowd to make people fall in love. This Roman source shows eros in two specific ways outside Christianity: 'erotic love', the state of romantic love, and 'eroticism', the thought or acting out of sexual desire in pursuit of sexual arousal.

Two thousand years ago, the Greeks had a very different view of eros, and this earlier view, adopted by Christianity from the Hellenistic tradition and developed over the centuries, is now a discrete type of love within Christianity.

Plato views lovers as those in pursuit of their good, but when in concert with eros he sees them in pursuit of their highest good. This is not a perfect life with a perfect person. Plato looks beyond life. It is the lover's transcendental good that is everlasting — based on a philosophical understanding of beauty as a state of both being beautiful and knowing beauty. Plato's view, when applied to his philosophical extreme, is one he thinks everyone loves and seeks to possess, whether they realise it or

---

[XXXVIII] Christians are inspired to believe in the virtue of hope as defined in the Catechism of the Catholic Church, published by the Vatican in 1822. Hope is the theological virtue by which we desire the Kingdom of Heaven and eternal life as our happiness, placing our trust in Christ's promises and relying not on our own strength, but on the help of the grace of the Holy Spirit. Source: http://www.vatican.va

not. After all, who does not want to possess the highest good?

Plato's highest good is ascension on death to an overworld with the Godhead as an intellectual equal — a place of immersion in beauty, where the dead are beautiful in spirit, and all-knowing in the same way as the Godhead[171]. This platonic view of the afterlife as a highest good includes three concepts, which Christianity has adopted and adapted:

The first is our overwhelming desire to possess the highest good so that we strive to seek and possess it in perpetuity. To achieve such, the lover takes abstracted ownership of the highest good as an ideal, bestows immense value upon it, and works towards it as a posture of attendance and tending. In Christian terms, the ideal loved and sought is to be with God and to see God[XXXIX] in the eternal afterlife by God's salvation and grace.[XL] The interpretation of this and of God's salvation and grace varies between Christian denominations and interpretations. Basically, Christians seek an afterlife of eternal highest good where they only know as much as God allows.

The second point is the ascension of the soul to the afterlife by good deeds in life. According to Plato, only by ascending five incremental steps — the *scala amoris* — culminating in total love of all things will the lover's soul enter the eternal afterlife and achieve the highest good.[172]

Although Christianity does not recognise Plato's *scala amoris*, the idea of ascension — via the *ordo salutis*, for example — is an essential view of many Christian sects: to enter the afterlife of highest good one must ascend towards it through a process that

---

[XXXIX] The concept of seeing God in Christian terms is one of debate, depending on the interpretation of Christian scripture. For many, seeing God after death is not seeing in a physical way, but in intellectual terms, whereby the believer finally and resolutely understands Him in an afterlife rich in His presence. This interpretation seems to have direct links to Plato's description of an afterlife of ultimate beauty, where the lover does not see beauty but understands it in intellectual terms.

[XL] There is a distinction drawn between the love of God (vertical philia) and the love of being with God (eros). During the Middle Ages, this distinction seems to have been made when the Christian is denied merger with God. Prior to this, a single love would have sufficed, as to love God and end in a state of merger with God required a single love object, God.

includes good deeds in life[XLI].

In Plato's view, the first step on the way to ascension — ultimate beauty — is the love of aesthetic perfection, specifically between two beautiful lovers. The lover must know and accept an ideal of love that includes aesthetic beauty, and then find and possess that perfect beautiful beloved. The beloved may be male or female — gender did not matter. Then there are two possibilities:

- ♥ The lover has beautiful children with his beautiful beloved as a means to achieve eternal yet existential existence through his progeny
- ♥ The lover bestows love upon a beautiful boy, in the Athenian practice of *uranian paiderasteia*, and passes on wisdom and virtue. His philosophical teachings are passed on in perpetuity under the same doctrine by the boy as he matures.[XLII]

In both cases, the lover takes on the love of a beautiful beloved under the framework of the *scala amoris*, and achieves immortality through children and/or bestowed wisdom and virtue.

The next step is to bestow love on all people without jealousy as love becomes independent of individuals and is spread across people in general.

The third step is recognition and bestowed love upon the beautiful minds of people, when the aesthetic of any single individual within society becomes irrelevant. Plato stresses this idea of ignoring the aesthetic of all beloveds. Outward

---

[XLI] As outlined in The New Schaff-Herzog Encyclopaedia of Religious Knowledge, Vol. VIII: Morality – Petersen by Philip Schaff (circa 1850) chapter: Order of Salvation online available at:
http://www.ccel.org/s/schaff/encyc/encyc08/htm/ii.vii.htm#ii.vii.

[XLII] *Uranian paiderasteia* was practised by Athenians at this time, offering eternal existence to the lover by handing on wisdom and virtue to a youth, now a man himself, who lives on when the lover ascends to the afterlife of all knowing forms. In Athenian society it was broadly accepted for a man to have a sexual or platonic relationship with a male youth,. It is believed Plato himself was critical of sexual pederasty, and within the *scala amoris* his intent is clearly platonic only.

appearance becomes generally irrelevant, and instead wisdom, virtue, passion and love are the things of beauty. The lover must seek these attributes and love all beloveds who display them. Where wisdom, virtue, passion and love are absent, the lover must instil them through philosophical teaching.

In loving all souls, the lover is ready to move on to the penultimate step of the *scala amoris*: bestowed love upon the beauty of state institutions and law. At this point, the lover loves all that humankind is, from the single in aesthetic beauty to the many in the beauty of mind, and from the beauty of all souls to the beauty of all as a body politic. These loves form the whole of humanity within nature, which we consider today as the humanities.

Plato's final step — only achievable as the lover's life ends — is to gain an in-depth appreciation with bestowed love of Nature herself. Such complete existential knowledge is what Plato refers to as the single science that in his day included not only the humanities, but mathematics, astronomy, biology, medicine, philosophy and logic. It is at this point of knowing all beyond self that the lover understands existential beauty. Once understood and love bestowed, the lover is ready for emersion into an overworld of ultimate, transcendental, eternal beauty. As Diotima explains:

> *"...and to understand that the beauty of them all is of one family, and that personal beauty is a trifle; and after laws and institutions he will go on to the sciences, that he may see their beauty, being not like a servant in love with the beauty of one youth or man or institution, himself a slave mean and narrow-minded, but drawing towards and contemplating the vast sea of beauty, he will create many fair and noble thoughts and notions in boundless love of wisdom; until on that shore he grows and waxes strong, and at last the vision is revealed to him of a single science, which is the science of beauty everywhere."*[173]

Plato's *scala amoris* is a lover's progress to enlightenment. It begins with love's bestowal of beauty upon the highest good and then follows a journey from micro-love to macro-love, ending in the lover's ascent to transcendental existence.

In broad Christian terms, eros is also a lover's progress that begins with the bestowal of love upon a destination of beauty as the highest good. In this case, the highest good is the Kingdom of Heaven, a place of everlasting existence with God.[XLIII/174] Like Plato's *scala amoris* it also includes good deeds here on earth to support the lover's progress. For some Christian sects, this may be through clearly laid out progressive steps such as the *ordo salutis*. For others, demonstrable deed may be less formal and merely include the adoption of doctrine, including acceptance of the Word, the love of God and Jesus Christ, and the practice of Christian Charity.[XLIV/175]

Plato's third point of highest good for the lover on ascension is all-knowing. This is the beauty Diotima speaks of once the lover achieves the pinnacle of the *scala amoris*.

Such pursuit of the highest good by the lover introduces several secondary conditions in platonic eros love. First: *my love is predicated on ascendance via my journey along the scala amoris, which results in my earthly immortality through progeny and/or paiderasteia and possession of everlasting wisdom achieved by my emersion into absolute transcendental beauty.*

The wisdom in Plato's secondary condition is specific: *I will be immortal of mind in Heaven where I will be all-knowing, and immortal of body through progeny and paiderasteia on earth.* As ascension is the highest good sought and loved by Plato, all bestowals of love within the *scala amoris* are under the condition they bring the lover closer to the ideal he loves. This has two implications:

[XLIII] "The fruits of Charity are joy, peace, and mercy; Charity demands beneficence and fraternal correction; it is benevolence; it fosters reciprocity and remains disinterested and generous; it is friendship and communion.: Love is itself the fulfilment of all our works. There is the goal; that is why we run: we run toward it, and once we reach it, in it we shall find rest." Source: http://www.vatican.va

[XLIV] Charity is the theological virtue by which we love God above all things for his own sake, and our neighbour as ourselves for the love of God. Source: http://www.vatican.va

1. The lover bestows love upon people and things within the *scala amoris* to achieve his highest good.
2. If he stops believing in ascension, he will withdraw his love from the ideal of ascension and the people and things he loves within the *scala amoris*.

Another secondary condition of Plato's eros love is acceptance that: *on my ascension, through my embrace of the scala amoris, I will love the overworld I find myself in, a place of my everlasting knowing with the all-knowing.*

Christianity does not subscribe to either of these two secondary conditions of platonic eros love. The first suggests:

1. By following the path to ascension, ascension is inevitable.
2. Absolute possession of perfect knowledge in the overworld is achievable.

The former is at odds with God's overarching choice to bring the lover into Heaven. Nowhere in Diotima's account does she suggest denial of access to the overworld, but for the Christian, denial is always possible.

The latter would be a contradiction with the Adam and Eve allegory laid out in *Genesis*. Adam takes a small part of the wisdom of God from the Tree of Life on pain of punishment: that of knowing good and evil.[XLV/176] Therefore, God implies that not all of His knowledge is Adam's to take. Since no biblical text states that humanity can in any way be equal to God in His omniscient knowledge of the existential or transcendental, for the Christian there can be no search for ultimate knowledge, although there can be a search for wisdom deemed proper by God for humans to have. Knowing this, the Christian accepts

---

[XLV] And the LORD God said, Behold, the man is become as one of us, to know good and evil: and now, lest he put forth his hand, and take also of the tree of life, and eat, and live for ever: 3:23 Therefore the LORD God sent him forth from the garden of Eden, to till the ground from whence he was taken. Genesis 3:1-23

God on unequal terms.[XLVI/177] The eros love Plato bestows upon the highest good in pursuit of such good is not possible for the Christian.

Nevertheless, Christianity has succeeded in achieving a synthesis of platonic eros as the Christian is offered a version of the highest good beyond life. That highest Christian good is a place of everlasting joy, peace, mercy and love — one where the lover discards their mortal existence and is cleansed of their sins, God willing. This is God's Kingdom of Heaven, a place that is pure and infused with His love.

Eros love marks the start of the Christian's ascent when he or she joins the fellowship. The object of love is the Kingdom of Heaven that offers eternal joy, peace and mercy in the everlasting presence of God. This is the lover's highest good, similar to Plato's highest good. With bestowal in place, the committed lover embarks on a lifelong progressive journey. The Christian lover, unlike the platonic lover, does not seek to understand all humanities and sciences by the end of their journey. They seek immersion in Christianity, and trust in God to support them in joy, peace and mercy, granting His love through redemption.

In taking up Christian eros, the lover accepts the secondary conditions of: *my eros love is one of loving the ideal of Heaven everlasting with God as an ascension through Christian doctrine.*

This secondary condition also needs a further condition of acceptance: *my abstracted possession of the highest good will not be the possession of God, nor knowing the quintessential like God in His knowing. Rather, the highest good is a place for me in Heaven where I may see God and may be with Him, immersed in joy, peace, mercy and His love.*

This sets out the highest good Christians seek to achieve through eros love, that of citizenship of the Kingdom of Heaven.

[XLVI] Then shall the soul know God even as she is known: I Cor.XIII, r o. Then shall she love as she is loved; and over his Bride shall rejoice the Bridegroom, knowing and known, loving and beloved, Jesus Christ Our Lord, who is over all things, God blessed for ever. Amen. In Cant. Cant., Sermo LXXXII, 7 and 8.

Chapter 20

Philia

In everyday use philia is a suffix describing love or passion. Oenophilia is love of wine, anthropophilia is love of people or society, and theophilia is love of God.

According to Aristotle 2,300 years ago, philia was the mutual concern for the welfare of virtuous equal platonic lovers (someone like oneself).[XLVII/178] Such concern for equal lovers has been integrated into Christianity to bind followers emotionally within a given fellowship. Once bound, all members of the fellowship, who agree to its doctrine and spiritual equality, find meaning in Christianity. In doing so, they renounce worldly competition between one another through the equality of philia, and together defend and compete as one mind against a world of scarce resources. The result is a 'strength in numbers movement' within a proven hostile world of families, clans, other religious denominations, secular states, kingdoms and empires, and other actors who seek to assert their will over the fellowship.

Over centuries, Christianity has built on this idea of binding philia to such a degree that it now includes a horizontal and a vertical aspect covering the relationships between like-minded believers of God — fellowship love — and the relationship between each follower and God — love of God.

[XLVII] A virtuous person loves the recognition of himself as virtuous; to have a close friend is to possess yet another person, besides oneself, whose virtue one can recognise at extremely close quarters; therefore, it must be desirable to have someone very much like oneself whose virtuous activity one can perceive (IX 11). *Aristotle Nicomachean Ethics.*

Fellowship Love (Horizontal Philia)
Fellowship love in a traditional sense is one where spiritually equal members of the fellowship bestow love upon one another. In doing so, followers bind to each other and their shared faith, take up the fellowship's doctrine and disseminate it in a similar way to Internet-based news servers. Whenever they can, they reach out and connect, hold on to doctrinal information pertinent to their fellowship, take on the same from trusted sources and share doctrine verbatim with any requestors. The result is a bound whole that includes a cohesive and highly resilient shared network of ideas.

Christianity has developed and refined a network of people sharing ideas throughout the world and over millennia as a means to not only hold, maintain and share doctrine, but to bind followers to each other and the faith. In this way, fellowship love is a love between those who know their beloveds with a high degree of intimacy (their local network) and those who know their beloveds to a lesser degree (their regional, national and multinational network) although, regardless of intimacy, all followers share love and a common doctrine that is clear and distinct.

It is doubtful Christianity consciously adopted fellowship love. It probably embraced the human inclination of birds of a feather flocking together within the idea of Aristotelian virtuous equals. Christianity seems also to have blended Charity[XLVIII] with birds of a feather, resulting in the Christian fellowship love we see today.[XLIX/179]

In a practical sense, fellowship love is beyond race, country, tribe, family, gender or any other sameness that defines other

---

[XLVIII] Charity as defined in the Catechism of the Catholic Church (1822) published by the Vatican is "the theological virtue by which we love God above all things for his own sake, and our neighbour as ourselves for the love of God." Source Http://www.vatican.va

[XLIX] We are bound to thank God always for you, brethren, as it is meet, because that your faith groweth exceedingly, and the charity of every one of you all toward each other aboundeth. The Second Epistle of Paul the Apostle to the Thessalonians 1:3

birds of a feather beyond the fellowship. The loving bond created between followers results in the love of all by all. Such love is regardless of whom a follower may be, where they may be, or the level of intimacy between them. And yet, in spite of achieving such a binding love across the fellowship, the followers themselves take on a posture of hostility towards outsiders where they feel under threat, regardless of common attributes that might bind them.

It is this model of inner strength and outer hostility that differentiates fellowship love from Christian Charity. Freud suggested that religious affiliations, like loyal armies, become intolerant and at times cruel to those who are not of the same fellowship.[L/180] Charity on the other hand, according to Catholicism, is the bestowal of love upon all people, regardless of any and all difference between them, based on God's infusion of love in all things.[181]

The lyrics of the hymn *Onward, Christian Soldiers*, offer an excellent example of the nature of Christian groups bound by fellowship love:

> *Onward, Christian soldiers, marching as to war,*
> *With the cross of Jesus going on before.*
> *Christ, the royal Master, leads against the foe;*
> *Forward into battle see His banners go!*[182]

This first verse extols the army that marches into battle against 'the foe' under Christ's banner. The foe are Christ's and God's enemies. As a consequence, this army will vanquish those who do not consider Christ their royal Master.

The hymn glorifies the Crusades as a holy war and pays homage to those who fought under Christ's banner from 1095 through to the 16th century.[183]

The moment you bestow love upon the fellowship, all members of the fellowship bestow love upon you. As this

---

[L] Therefore, a religion, even if it calls itself a religion of love, must be hard and unloving to those who do not belong to it. Fundamentally every religion is a religion of love for all those it embraces, while cruelty and intolerance towards those who do not belong to it are natural to every religion.

happens, you accept the conditions of reciprocation which include not only the uptake of church doctrine, but a bond so tight that it leads to intolerance of those outside the fellowship, regardless of the underlying message of Charity the fellowship espouses to under the broader Christian message. Where the doctrine calls for Charity for all, it also requires hostile resistance to anyone trying to devalue, bring harm to or destroy the body politic of the fellowship.

A secondary condition intimately linked these points is *unconditional acceptance to think and do righteously following the fellowship's doctrine.*

This is clear in the video documentary of the Christian *Peoples Temple* cult tragedy. Members of the cult loved wholeheartedly and took on doctrine with all the duties expected. Under a perceived threat from U.S. government human rights investigators, they gunned down five of the visiting government officials and all but a few of the sect committed suicide by drinking cyanide-laced grape juice. Nine hundred and nine died that day in Jonestown, including 304 children.[184]

Beyond these secondary conditions, there are two significant problems in accepting fellowship love as a valid love type. How to have an intimate and meaningful relationship with a faceless body politic?

And although the lover bestows love upon each follower as an equal to all others, all fellowships are hierarchical.

In terms of equality, the lover accepts the 'sameness' of each follower regardless of place within the hierarchy. To the Christian, all are fallen and all are believers in God and doctrine. To love one is to love all, provided each remains within the fellowship.

The status of individuals up and down the hierarchy is outside the lover's veil of assent. Position is not relevant to the perfect-imperfect of the followers who belong to the same fellowship when they are all equally fallen and equally believe. This idea of equality in terms of fallen and belief is further harmonized by God's love, which is not bestowed in terms of Church hierarchy. His love, agapē is bestowed without favour.

The lover need not be intimately involved with any of the

fellowship since everyone within it is one and the same. The lover mentally creates one abstracted follower, a platonic form of the perfect beloved Christian or an identity mosaic of the perfect-imperfect beloved using the veil of assent. The lover then abstractly owns this Christian and views all sect members as one and the same under one body politic.

As the lover bestows love upon the fellowship as a body of beloveds, the fellowship takes up ownership of the lover as their beloved and accepts the lover into the fellowship with their bestowed love, which in essence incorporates the lover into the body politic.

Christian scripture suggests God made all equal and loves equally where He wills, regardless of place in the fellowship. It is this sense of emotional oneness between the lover and the fellowship that is at the root of fellowship love's appraisal and bestowal.

Love of God (Vertical Philia)

For some Christian sects, a single and direct bestowal of love upon God is sufficient. In others the lover must love the Trinity of the Father, the Son, and the Holy Spirit.[185] This subtle but significant difference is down to the nature of God either as one entity in His own right or an entity comprising three as one.

Vertical philia is the love of God as one or as the Trinity.

Christianity dictates that you must love God: "*Jesus said unto Him* [the lawyer of the Pharisees] *Thou shalt love the Lord thy God with all thy heart, and with all thy soul, and with all thy mind. This is the first and great commandment.*"[186]

In terms of authenticity, God would not demand your love if such love were inauthentic, so the lover considers God of immense value, assuredly commits to attend and tend to Him, and takes abstracted ownership of Him, either solely or as the Trinity.

The ardent lover sets no conditions on God when loving Him. Their love is unconditional as God would expect — as laid out in the story of *Job* or out of frui following St. Augustine, where the lover loves God simply because He is.[LI/187]

This does not mean the lover's bestowal of love is unconditional in absolute terms. The lover can at any time withdraw their love from God. Where the lover moves from Christianity to another faith that excludes the Christian God, they will withdraw their love, and similarly if the lover rejects faith altogether they will turn their back on God. Therefore the lover's love is bound to their continuance of the Christian faith.

Some people doubt the validity of this kind of love. The merit of a relationship between a human lover and an omnipotent supernatural God where human love includes intimacy, equality and liberty stretches credibility. And for those who reject God's existence entirely, there can be no vertical philia.

The scripture demands that believers love God. Any qualities of intimacy, equality, liberty and God's omnipotence are irrelevant. The lover loves, as Matthew tells them to do when he quotes Jesus, with all their heart, soul and mind regardless of these qualities.[LII] They do so religiously with one overriding condition: *an ongoing belief in God's existence*. Within this context, love of God is a valid love type to the believer within the three-pillar model.

[LI] God proves to Satan that Job's love is born of benevolence, not out of favour or fear.

[LII] The Lord our God is one Lord: / And thou shalt love the Lord thy God with all thy heart, and with all thy soul, and with all thy mind, and with all thy strength: this is the first commandment. Mark 12:30.

Chapter 21

Agapē

In *The Merchant of Venice*, Portia explains mercy to Shylock to avoid his cutting a pound of flesh from Antonio's breast. Her *quality of mercy* speech describes agapē with precision as God's bestowal of love upon good and evil people alike.[188] It descends like rain from heaven, and is the greatest force for mercy towards all people by all people. God bestows agapē without favour and everyone He loves recognizes that they too must bestow their love upon God[LIII/189] and all others (through Charity) upon whom God has also bestowed agapē.[LIV/190]

In a contemporary setting, *The Power of Love* by Frankie Goes to Hollywood describes agapē as a force from God that first creates beauty and then cleanses the soul through redemption. Agapē inhibits thoughts of selfish desires, or sublimates them to adoration for God.

Agapē is also protection from supernatural threats and misfortune. It is eternal in terms of its ability to defy death, and is a love bestowed regardless of impurity. According to the song, agapē infuses purity, in that God's love is imbued with divine purity, or as much as can permeate the eternally fallen.[191]

The first of the four features that distinguish agapē from all other love types is spontaneity at the point of the beloved's

---

[LIII] We love him, because he first loved us. John I 4:19.

[LIV] Beloved, if God so loved us, we ought also to love one another. No man hath seen God at any time. If we love one another, God dwelleth in us, and his love is perfected in us. John I 4:11-12.

creation.

Human love is not spontaneous, because love's bestowal as a verb is rational. You choose who is worthy of your love, as your decision to love is based on your pursuit and possession of the good. Agapē does not work this way as the sheer fact of existence brought about by God is enough to receive agapē.

Second, agapē is indifferent to beloved value. God, when radiating agapē, does not seek out the perfect for possession or consider one person of greater value than another in the way human lovers do through appraisal. [LV/192]

The third feature in agapē is value creating itself. Nothing is of value without the bestowal of God's love. This means you cannot love anything without God's love first, as all value is God-given through agapē. Nothing and nobody but God can create initial value — and God does not seek good or the perfect, He creates it:

> *And God saw everything that He had made, and, behold, it was very good.*[193]
>
> Genesis 1:31

It is this good manifested as value, which you pursue and ultimately possess on your bestowal of love upon all beloveds so that your good is a function of God's good, as God creates everything and makes it good through agapē.

Finally, agapē initiates the love of God by the Christian,[LVI/194] creating a circuit of love where His love returns to Him through His bestowal of love upon the Christian. God's creation is imbued with His love, without which it could not love Him.

Although agapē is different to the other love types, it meets

---

[LV] If God loves above and beyond agapē, this may suggest a downward vertical love of individual persons by God: "Judas saith unto him, not Iscariot, Lord, how is it that thou wilt manifest thyself unto us, and not unto the world? Jesus answered and said unto him: If a man love me, he will keep my words: and my Father will love him, and we will come unto him, and make our abode with him." John 14:22-23.

[LVI] We love him, because he first loved us. John I 4:19.

the necessary conditions for those who believe God exists: bestowal of value upon the beloved, even though such bestowal is spontaneous, unlike human love;[195] retained abstracted ownership,[LVII]/[196] according to the scriptures, although He may reduce us to a platonic form or a perfect-imperfect human; a posture of assured commitment to attend and tend in terms of support for life and after death.

Agapē is no different from any other love in terms of conditionality. If conditions are failed by the beloved, God may take back His love as He sees fit.[LVIII]

[LVII] In Hosea 24:1 through covenant, God is clear that 'Thou art my people' and in this, God does take abstracted ownership of followers within the covenant.

[LVIII] Job 1:21 The Lord gave, and the Lord hath taken away; blessed be the name of the Lord.

Chapter 22

Nomos

Singer defines nomos love as "*...love as righteousness, acceptance of God's law, humble submission to his will.*"[sic]197

A good citizen adopts and abides by their country's culture, acquiring knowledge of its beliefs, arts, morals, laws, customs, language and other attributes and habits shared by their society.198 Christianity and the laws of Christian countries tend to overlap, although they are incompatible with nomos love.

In its purest form, nomos is relinquishing one's own free will to God through the bestowal of love upon God's will as commanded to do so by His Word:

> *Servants, be obedient to them that are your masters according to the flesh, with fear and trembling, in singleness of your heart, as unto Christ; Not with eyeservice, as menpleasers; but as the servants of Christ, doing the will of God from the heart; With good will doing service, as to the Lord, and not to men: Knowing that whatsoever good thing any man doeth, the same shall he receive of the Lord, whether he be bond or free.*199
>
> Ephesians 6:5-8

Here, Paul tells the Ephesians to be as obedient to their masters as to Christ and by virtue as to God. He suggests that in pursuit of the good, they will receive good in measure from God, who wants Christians to do His bidding without question because His bidding is always good when loved.

Nomos is deeper than righteousness, moral upstanding and piousness in reverence to God. To love God's will wholeheartedly is to relinquish free will forever within a state of total submission for all that God is and all that God wants.

Jesus tells the scribe "*The Lord our God is one Lord: / And thou shalt love the Lord thy God with all thy heart, and with all thy soul, and with all thy mind, and with all thy strength: this is the first commandment.*"[200]

The Word of God tells the Christian to submit all of their heart, soul, mind and strength to Him in absolute unquestioning adoration in pursuit of His highest good when alive, and from beyond the grave. This is a good above all other goods to value, and in doing so you take abstracted possession of God's will through unquestioning bestowal of love.

To achieve such submission to God's will you must first discard your own free will forever, regardless of the consequences. Second you must submit wholeheartedly and unquestioningly to the perpetual influence of God's will, choosing to enter a realm you will never leave or question, regardless of all good or bad as seen by others.

Popular media wrongly portray nomos as pious characters driven by fanatical righteousness, but this is not how Christianity interprets it. In Tarantino's 1994 movie *Pulp Fiction*, Jules, a gangster, is about to kill Ringo during an armed robbery. As he points his gun at Ringo, he misquotes *Ezekiel* 25:17.[201]

The passage refers to God's punishment of the evil and selfish, and how this contrasts with the righteous man whom God blesses for his or her acts of Charity and goodwill. Jules recites this to show his blind acceptance of a Godhead's will within an ideology.

The film is about Jules' submission to Marsellus' will in contrast to Christian morality, and his later redemption after a near-death experience.

The passage Tarantino uses illustrates the righteous people leading the weak between the tempting slopes of the selfish on one side and the evil on the other. Where the righteous and the weak stay on the valley floor, Jules as the hand of God/Marsellus spares them vengeance, but those who stray — the enemies of Marsellus' syndicate — he avenges through Jules.

Jules' role is as a tool of the Godhead/Marsellus, so that he acts in reverence of Marsellus' vengeance becoming a moral killing tool of the mob Godhead by misapplying Christian nomos.

His spiritual awakening and rejection of Marsellus' will is the modern interpretation of righteousness, where the sinner suddenly sees the error of their ways and seeks redemption. For Jules this is achieved by dropping to the valley floor and leading Ringo, the weak, out of temptation.

However, nomos is the full and unquestioning adoption of God's will where there is no release or redemption for any acts done in His name: *God's will is perfect, and I submit to it wholeheartedly.*

Where God demanded the sacrifice of Isaac for example, his father Abraham obeyed unquestioningly and would have killed his son through his obedience to God's will had He had not ordered him to stop.[202] Nomos is an ideal with no grounds for the revocation of bestowed love upon God's will.

If Abraham were alive today his extremist, nomos love would be in direct conflict with human cultures, and laws. Western laws seek democratic justice for all. The American cry for inalienable rights of life, liberty and the pursuit of happiness and the French maxim liberté, égalité, fraternité are both reminders of these values, guaranteeing rights of life, freedom to think and act, and equality of race and ethnicity, but God's law, through His Word, relies on His principles alone. These are often contradictory. When Jesus says to the Devil in Matthew 4:10: "*...for it is written, thou shalt worship the Lord thy God, and Him only shalt thou serve,*" it is understood that Christians must worship God and serve only Him. Secular law is incompatible with this as it guarantees freedom of belief including disbelief and rejection of service to God. Anyone taking up nomos condemns secular law for being contrary to God's Word.

If God enforces His will and has those who bestow love upon nomos dismantle human laws, and punishes those who follow them, he causes holy war? If He accepts human law, he disregards His own Word, where secularism is present and His will is unsatisfied.

Nomos is a valid love type, but in reality it is an unachievable existential wide-ideal lifestyle where the lover bestows immense value upon God's will as God's Word, because the lover holds

God's will in reverence. The lover assures commitment to attend and tend by taking up the deeds and duties of the Word and abstracted ownership of the perfection of God's will. The lover loves for the same reason all lovers love: the possession of the good in terms of sacrifice to God as the scriptures demand.

The lover takes on the secondary condition of bestowing nomos love by foregoing free will to God unquestioningly, which assumes the lover's unreserved belief in God, and that God is the one who seeks the lover's nomos love.

However as the lover takes up this condition, they have no means to regain self-control, although they can at any time withdraw their bestowal of love. Some lovers may consider it wrong to submit to God's will and then backtrack but, right or wrong, they do not entirely lose free will on submission, even if they deny themselves such in pursuit of losing themselves to Him.

Glossary and Terms

Abstracted ownership—*noun*: the psychological uptake of ownership by the lover of the beloved in a way that respects the freedom of the beloved legitimately and morally.

Appraisal—*verb*: the determination by the prospective lover or lover of the prospective beloved, or beloved to bestow love or maintain ongoing bestowed love. For those falling in love appraisal comprises initial appraisal, which precedes the dating relationship, followed by appraisal prior to bestowed love. Once in love, the lover maintains an ongoing posture of appraisal ensuring needs are met, rights respected and values over the life of the loving relationship.

Attachment—*noun*: emotional closeness to another person or thing. Attachment is not necessarily a consistent feeling, rather the idea that separation from the person or object attached to brings on anxiety to the person who is attached.

Being in Love—1/2. *verb/noun*: the second phase of romantic love's progress after *falling in love* and preceding *staying in love*. see *In love*.

Bestowal (of love)—*verb*: the lover's announcement, either spoken or conveyed through their actions or thought, signifying the entrance into the state of being in love.

Cognitive—1. *noun*: the conscious thought area that processes thought, particularly rational thought. 2. *adjective*: thought, particularly rationally, occurring in the cognitive area.

Commitment (assured)—*noun*: at the conscious layer of the three-pillar model, the lover takes on a committed posture of being there for the beloved wherever and whenever (as agreed and expected). At the emotional layer the lover, through interaction with the beloved, takes up an emotional sense of concern (see *robust concern*) for the beloved where they think and act in a way consistent with concern for the beloved's welfare.

Community of two—*noun*: as lover and beloved come closer through appraisal, they focus on each other to the exclusion of those around them, but this is not the same as rejecting others. Lovers, particularly romantic lovers, do and say things privately that remain between them, while enjoying the company of other people and bringing up children. In essence, the lovers take on a sense of micro-culture where they share beliefs, habits, morality, and views.

Conative—1. *noun*: subconscious thought area associated with emotion, drive and desire. 2. *adjective*: emotional, driven or desirous precursive ideas presented to the cognitive area of the mind for action.

Fellowship—*noun*: a body of followers of a particular religious group, Roman Catholicism for example.

Form—*noun*: the quintessential object of all objects in the same set. Forms are a philosophical idea of purity that extend beyond physical objects to concepts of beauty, honour, virtue, etc.

Frui—1. *adjective*: on a continuum between uti and frui, where a loving relationship is described as 'frui skewed', the lover considers their benefits from the relationship are of lesser concern than the beloved's. 2. *noun*: a frui loving relationship is one with altruistic characteristics (see adjective 1.)

Good (the)—*noun*: the subjective view of both net benefit and loving sentiment by the lover or potential lover. The lover gains a sense of the good by asking if life has been beneficial so far with the beloved, is it now and will it be in the future, and a summing up of sentiment with the beloved. So the lover has a view of the presence and extent of the good perceived.

Hybrid—1. *adjective*: on a continuum between uti and frui, where a loving relationship is described as hybrid the lover considers their benefits from the relationship are of equal concern to the beloved's. 2. *noun*: A hybrid loving relationship is one with hybrid characteristics (see adjective 1.)

Identity mosaic—*noun*: the set of all known attributes of a person, held in the mind and ordered by cluster and importance.

In love—1. *verb*: The lover's posture of assured commitment to attend and tend to the beloved and abstractly own them, and a perception of immense value in the beloved which is bestowed upon the beloved. 2. *noun*: a state of love whereby the lover loves the beloved. For romantic relationships both the verb and noun can be prefixed by *falling*, *being* or *staying* to determine the phase of love the lover is in.

Love (adjective)—*adjective*: a description of the lover's state of mind, usually expressing sentiment of feelings.

Love (verb)—*verb*: the posture taken up by the lover whereby there is assured commitment to attend and tend to the beloved, bestowed immense value and abstracted ownership of the beloved.

Loving sentiment—*noun*: the aggregate sentiment of how the lover feels about the beloved, or prospective beloved based on time spent and time anticipated together.

Media—*noun*: film, song, literature, television programming including fiction and non-fiction that reflects Western culture. In contrast to news media.

Necessary conditions—*noun*: universal attributes of love that must be present for love to exist. These include immense value bestowed, assured commitment to attend and tend, and abstracted ownership of the beloved as defined in the three-pillar model.

Perfect-imperfect—*noun*: the lover's perception of the beloved once they accept all flaws by means of the Stradivarius effect and veil of assent mechanisms.

Robust concern—*verb*: desirous (volitional) concern for the beloved insomuch as concern is not in the conscious layer of the cognitive mind, but the emotional layer of the conative mind.

Romantic intimacy—*noun*: a state of emotional closeness between a couple who are either romantically dating or romantically in love.

Romanticism—*noun*: a contextual backdrop comprising elements synonymous with Romanticism (idolization, heroes and damsels, fusion, safe harbour and everlasting love).

Secondary conditions—*noun*: a lover's selective need, right or value that must be present in a loving relationship.

Social Cognitive Theory—*adjective*: an individual's knowledge and action is related to external observation of others when interacting with the world and immersed in media. Specifically, roleplay is a function of upbringing, interaction with others across culture and observations of media.

Staying in love—1/2. *verb/noun*: the third and final phase of romantic love's progress after *being in love* (see *In love*).

Stradivarius effect—*noun*: mechanism that supports the lover's creation of the perfect-imperfect beloved by accepting imperfect attributes of the beloved's identity into the beloved's identity mosaic. Usually used in conjunction with the veil of assent (see *Veil of assent*).

Three-pillar model—*noun*: three-columned, three-rowed model showing how all loving relationships are created from the lower emotional row, reasoned at the central row and rationalized at the top row, and how love is sustainable between the lover and the love object when all elements are present and stable.

Uti—*adjective*: on a continuum between uti and frui, where a loving relationship is described as 'uti skewed' the lover considers their benefits from the relationship are of greater concern than the beloved's. 2. *noun*: an uti loving relationship is one with egoistic characteristics (see adjective 1.)

Value (beloved)—*noun*: exceeding objective and buyer value, the lover recognizes *beloved value* through firsthand appraisal of the beloved and appreciates the good achieved in the relationship based on net benefits and loving sentiment (see *Good (the)* and *Loving sentiment*).

Veil of assent—*noun*: mechanism that supports the lover's creation of the perfect-imperfect by filtering out non-applicable attributes of the beloved's identity from the beloved's identity mosaic. Usually used in conjunction with the Stradivarius effect.

Notes and References

[1] Lewis. C. S. *The Four Loves*. 1960, Harcourt Brace & Company. ISBN:0-15-132916-8

[2] Shakespeare. W. *Romeo and Juliet*. 1595. Project Gutenberg. Available for download at: http://www.gutenberg.org keyword: Romeo and Juliet

[3] *Moulin Rouge!* Dir. Baz Luhrmann. Twentieth Century Fox. 2001. 44-55 minutes. Film. Available from Amazon.com

[4] May, S. *Love: A History*. 2011, Yale University Press. P.6 ISBN: 978-0-300-11830-8

[5] Sande, E. Where I Sleep. Sande, E. Khan, S. *Our Version of Events*. Virgin EMI 2010-11. Compact Disc. Available from iTunes and other online retailers keyword: Where I Sleep

[6] de Botton, A. *On Love*. 1993. Grove Press, New York. ISBN: 0-8021-3409-02

[7] Lewis, T. Amini, F. Lannon, R. *A General Theory of Love*. 2000, Vintage Books, Random House Publishing. pp. 63-64. ISBN: 978-0-375-70922-7

[8] Ibid., pp. 78-81

[9] Adele. Crazy for You. Adkins, A.. *19*. XL records. 2016. Compact Disc. Available from iTunes and other online retailers keyword: Crazy for You

[10] Tallis. F. *Love Sick*. 2004. Random House Group, London. p.2 ISBN: 0-7126-2904-1

[11] Ibid.

[12] Tennov, D. *Love and Limerence. The Experience of Being in Love*. 1999. Scarborough House, MD. pp.4-5. ISBN: 0-8128-6286-4

[13] Rihanna. We All Want Love. Dean. Wilson, E. Wyreman, S. Randolph, K. Gonzales. *Talk That Talk*. DefJam Music. 2011. Compact Disk. Available from iTunes and other online retailers keyword: We All Want Love

[14] Singer, I. *The Nature of Love, 1 Plato and Luther*. 2009, The MIT Press. p.6. ISBN: 978-0-262-51272-5

[15] Ibid., p.9

[16] Nat King Cole. (I Love You) For Sentimental Reasons. Watson, I (Deek). Best, W (Pat). *Unforgettable*. Capitol. 1954. Compact Disc. Available from iTunes and other online retailers keyword: (I Love You) For Sentimental Reasons

[17] Plato. *Symposium*. c385BC. Translation: Jowett, B. Project Gutenberg. Available for download at: http://www.gutenberg.org keyword: Symposium

[18] *Cinderella*. Dir. Kenneth Branagh. Disney. 2015. Film. Available from Amazon.com and other online retailers

[19] Frankfurt, H. *Necessity, Volition, and Love*, Cambridge: Cambridge University Press. 1999. pp129. ISBN 978-0521633956

[20] Ella Henderson. Hard Work. Henderson, E. Remi, S. *Chapter One*. Syco. Sony. 2014 Compact Disc. Available from iTunes and other online retailers keyword: Hard Work

[21] *The Notebook*. Dir. Nick Cassavetes. New Line. 2004. Film. Minutes 9-11. Available from Amazon.com and other online retailers

[22] Singer, I. *The Nature of Love, 1 Plato and Luther*. 2009, The MIT Press. p.7. ISBN: 978-0-262-51272-5

[23] *An Unmarried Woman*. Dir. Paul Mazursky. Twentieth Century Fox. 1798. Film. Available from Amazon.com and other online retailers

[24] Singer, I. *The Nature of Love, 1 Plato and Luther*. 2009, The MIT Press. p.7. ISBN: 978-0-262-51272-5

[25] Rihanna. *We All Want Love*.

[26] Adele. Water Under the Bridge. Adkins, A. Kurstin, G. *25*. XL records. 2016. Compact Disc. Available from iTunes and other online retailers keyword: Water Under the Bridge

[27] *The Notebook*. 24-26 minutes

[28] American philosopher John Rawls devised a thought experiment in the mid-20th-century called the Original Position, which uses the idea of bringing forth and holding back information behind the Veil of Ignorance (Rawls, J. *A Theory of Justice*. 1999. Harvard University Press. ISBN 0-674-00078-1). The Original Position has been acknowledged as a device for social policy development around the world. And yet beyond Rawls' thought experiment defined in the nineteen-sixties, the idea of a Veil of

Ignorance (modified to the veil of assent here) has been used by lovers during appraisal and beyond for millennia.

[29] *Pretty Woman*. Dir. Garry Marshal. Touchstone Pictures. 1990. Film. Minutes 92-94. Available from Amazon.com and other online retailers

[30] Ibid., 113 minutes.

[31] Ibid., 91 minutes.

[32] This quote (La netteté d'esprit cause aussi la netteté de la passion; c'est pourquoi un esprit grand et net aime avec ardeur, et il voit distinctement ce qu'il aime) is widely attributed to the French mathematician and physicist Blaise Pascal (1623 – 1622). Direct reference to this quote in published works of Blaise Pascal, however, is not available

[33] *Titanic*. Dir. James Cameron. Twentieth Century Fox. 1997. Film. Available from Amazon.com and other online retailers

[34] Wagner, R. 1865. *Tristan und Isolde*. Opera. Königliches Hof- und Nationaltheater, Munich.

[35] Extract from the newspaper *The Era's* review of Wagner's first performance of *Tristan and Isolde* in London in 1882. Reference drawn from: Mander R. and Mitchenson J. (W.H. Allen, London, 1977), *The Wagner Companion* p.120

[36] *Tristan and Isolde*. Dir. Kevin Reynolds. Twentieth Century Fox. 2006. Film. Available from Amazon.com and other online retailers

[37] Keller, L. (Publication date unknown) *Tristan and Isolde*. Retrieved from http://www.urbancinefile.com.au/home/view.asp?a=11590&s=Reviews. Date retrieved. June 2015

[38] *Tristan and Isolde*. 42 minutes

[39] Shakespeare. W. *Romeo and Juliet*. 1595. Ebook. Project Gutenberg. Available for download at: http://www.gutenberg.org keyword: Romeo and Juliet

[40] Sleepless in Seattle. Dir. Nora Ephron. Tristar Pictures. 1993.Film. Minutes 18-22. Available to stream on YouTube.com and from Amazon.com and other online retailers

[41] Air Supply. *I Adore You*. (released as a single only) Hitchcock, R. Russell, G. EMI. 2015. Compact Disc. Available from iTunes and other online retailers keyword: Air Supply *I Adore You*

NOTES AND REFERENCES

[42] Miley Cyrus. Adore You. Barthe, S. Yoel, O. *Bangerz*. RCA. 2013. Compact Disc. Available from iTunes and other online retailers keyword: Adore You

[43] Jessie J. L.O.V.E.. Gad, T. Cornish. *Who You Are*. Lava Island Universal Republic. 2011 Compact Disc. Available from iTunes and other online retailers keyword: L.O.V.E.

[44] *Titanic* 162-165 minutes

[45] *Footloose*. Dir. Craig Brewer. Paramount Pictures. 2011. Film. Available from Amazon.com and other online retailers

[46] Ella Mae Bowen. Holding Out for a Hero. Steinman, J. Pitchford, D. *Footloose – Music from the Motion Picture 2011*. Atlantic Records. 2011. Compact Disc. Available from iTunes and other online retailers keyword: Ella Mae Bowen. Holding Out for a Hero

[47] Publius Ovidius Naso. *The Metamorphoses of Ovid, Books I-VII*. c8AD. Book The Fourth: Fable I. [IV.-166]. Translation: Riley, H.T. Project Gutenberg. Available for download at: http://www.gutenberg.org keyword: The Metamorphoses of Ovid.

[48] Ricky Martin. I Am Made of You. Rosa, R.D. Child, D. *Ricky Martin*. Columbia. 1999. Compact Disc. Available from iTunes and other online retailers keyword: I Am Made of You

[49] Celine Dion. Falling into You. Steinberg, B. Nowels, R. D'Ubaldo, M-C. *Falling into You*. Columbia. Epic. 1996. Compact Disc. Available from iTunes and other online retailers keyword: Falling into You

[50] Plato. *Symposium*. c385BC. Translation: Jowett, B. Aristophanes' speech. Project Gutenberg. Available for download at: http://www.gutenberg.org keyword: Symposium

[51] *What Dreams May Come*. Dir. Vincent Ward. Polygram Filmed Entertainment et al. 1998. Film. Available to stream on Youtube.com and from Amazon.com and other online retailers

[52] Meghan Trainor. Dear Future Husband. Trainor, M. Kadish. K.. *Title*. Epic 2015. Compact Disc. Available from iTunes and other online retailers keyword: Dear Future Husband

[53] Alicia Keys. Fallin'. Keys, A. *Songs in A Minor*. J. 2001. Compact Disc. Available from iTunes and other online retailers keyword: Fallin'

54 Shakespeare, W. *Romeo and Juliet* Act III. Scene V. Reflected in the 1996 movie *Rome and Juliet*. 82-86 Minutes

55 Sartre, J. Basic Writings. 2001. Routledge. pp.30-57. ISBN: 978-0-415-21368-4

56 *Le Mari De La Coiffeuse* [The Hairdresser's Husband] Dir. Patrice Leconte. Lambard Productions. 1990. Film. 46 - 48 Minutes. Available from Amazon.com and other online retailers

57 Christina Perri. Human. Perri, C. Johnson, M. *Head or Heart*. Atlantic Records. 2013. Compact Disc. Available from iTunes and other online retailers keyword: Human

58 Sartre, J. Basic Writings. 2001. Routledge. pp.30-57 ISBN: 978-0-415-21368-4; Sartre, J. Existentialism is a Humanism. 2007. Yale. pp. 17-35. ISBN: 978-0-300-11546-8

59 Yalom, I. D. *Love's Executioner – And Other Tales of Psychology*. Basic Books. pp. xi-xxiii. 2012. ISBN: 978-0-465-02011-9

60 May, S. *Love: A History*. P.6

61 *Exotica*. Dir. Atom Egoyan. Alliance Entertainment, et al. 1994. Film. 57-59 minutes. Available from Amazon.com and other online retailers

62 George Michael, Mutya Buena. This is Not Real Love. Michael, G. Jackman, J. Cushnan, R. *Twenty Five*. Sony BMG. 2006. Compact Disc. Available from iTunes and other online retailers keyword: This is Not Real Love

63 *Fatal Attraction*. Dir Adrian Lyne. Paramount Pictures. 1987. Film. 84-88 minutes. Available from Amazon.com and other online retailers

64 Singer, I., *The Nature of Love, 1 Plato and Luther*. 2009, The MIT Press. pp.344-355. ISBN: 978-0-262-51272-5. referencing: St. Augustine of Hippo. *Morals of the Catholic Church* in *Basic Writings of Saint Augustine*. c388AD

65 Bill Withers. Use Me. Withers, B. *Still Bill*. Sussex Records. 1972. Compact Disc. Available from iTunes and other online retailers keyword: Use Me

66 *Guys and Dolls*. Dir. Joseph L. Mankiewicz. Metro-Goldwyn-Mayer (MGM), 1955. Film. 100-105 minutes. Available from Amazon.com and other online retailers

⁶⁷ Ibid., 19-22 minutes

⁶⁸ Ibid., 44-48 minutes

⁶⁹ Ibid., 144-149 minutes

⁷⁰ Brontë, E. *Withering Heights*. EBook. Project Gutenberg. Available for download at: http://www.gutenberg.org keyword: Wuthering Heights. Also available in standard book from Amazon.com: ISBN: 0141439556

⁷¹ Eagles. Lyin' Eyes. Henley, D. Frey, G. *One of These Nights*. Asylum. 1975. Compact Disc. Available from iTunes and other online retailers keyword: Lyin' Eyes

⁷² *The Unbearable Lightness of Being*. Dir. Philip Kaufman. The Saul Zaentz Company, et al. 1998. Film. 41-43 minutes Available from Amazon.com and other online retailers

⁷³ *Othello*. Dir. Oliver Parker. Castle Rock Entertainment, et al. 1995. Film. 18-19 minutes. Available to stream on YouTube.com and from Amazon.com and other online retailers. (this is from Act I. Scene III of the original play available from Project Gutenberg. http://www.gutenberg.org keyword: Othello the Moor of Venice

⁷⁴ Ibid., 54-55 minutes (Act II. Scene III.)

⁷⁵ Ibid., 95-105 minutes (Act V Scene II.)

⁷⁶ Cyndi Lauper, Jonny Lang. How Blue Can You Get (AKA Downhearted). Feather, J. Feather, L. *Memphis Blues*. Downtown Records. 2010. Compact Disc. Available from iTunes and other online retailers keyword: Cyndi Lauper, Jonny Lang. How Blue Can You Get

⁷⁷ Fukuyama, F. *The End of History and the Last Man*. 1992. Harper Collins Books. pp. xvi-xvii, 162-170. ISBN: 0-380-72002-7

⁷⁸ *We Don't Live Here Anymore*. Dir. John Curan. Front Street Pictures, et al. 2004. Film. 61-67 minutes. Available from Amazon.com and other online retailers

⁷⁹ Ibid., 73-78 minutes

⁸⁰ The Beatles. Two of Us. Lennon, J. McCartney, P.. *Let It Be*. Apple Records. 1970. Compact Disc. Available from iTunes and other online retailers keyword: Two of Us

⁸¹ *Hannah and Her Sisters*. Dir. Woody Allen. Orion Pictures, et al. 1986.

Film 1-6 minutes. Available from Amazon.com and other online retailers

[82] Ibid., 43-48 minutes

[83] Ibid., 83-89 minutes

[84] *On Golden Pond*. Dir Mark Rydell. IPC Films, et al. 1981. Film 4 - 8 minutes. Available from Amazon.com and other online retailers

[85] Ibid., 91-93 minutes

[86] Ibid., 100-106 minutes

[87] van Gogh, V. *The Letters of Vincent van Gogh to His Brother, 1872-1886: Volumes I and II*. 1927, Constable & Co. ISIN B001VE4FGO. This preferred translation is from http://vangoghletters.org. available at: http://vangoghletters.org/vg/letters/let143/letter.html

[88] Nelson, P. *Defending the Devil: My Story as Ted Bundy's Last Lawyer*. 1994. William Morrow. p.319. ISBN: 978-0-688-10823-6

[89] Michaud, S. Ainsworth, H.. *The Only Living Witness: The True Account of Homicidal Insanity*. 1984. New American Library, Inc. p.249. ISBN: 0-451-12752-8

[90] Ibid., pp. 65-66

[91] Ibid., p. 300

[92] Ibid., pp. 308-309

[93] Hugo, V. *The Hunchback of Notre-Dame*. Webster's Thesaurus Edition. 2005 Icon Classics. p.182. ISBN: 0-497-25330-5

[94] *Hunchback of Notre-Dame*. Dir. Michael Tuchner. Columbia Pictures. 1982. Film. 13-15 minutes Available from Amazon.com and other online retailers

[95] Ibid.,70-75 minutes

[96] *Angel-A*. Dir. Luc Besson. EuropaCorp, et al. 2005. Film. 45-53 minutes. Available from Amazon.com and other online retailers

[97] *Single White Female*. Dir. Barbet Schroeder. Columbia Pictures, et al. 1992. Film. 53-54 minutes. Available from Amazon.com and other online retailers

[98] Ibid., 90-93 minutes

[99] *Angel-A.*, 60-65 minutes

[100] Luther Vandross. Dance with My Father. L. Marx, R. *Dance with My Father*. EMI Music Publishing, Chrysalis Music Group. 2003. Compact Disc. Available from iTunes and other online retailers keyword: Dance with My Father

[101] Kinsey, A. Pomeroy, W,B. Martin, C,E. Gebhard, P, H. *Sexual Behavior in the Human Female and Sexual Behavior in the Human Male.* Two Volume Set: 1953. W.B. Saunders. ISBN: 0-253-33412-8 & 0-253-33411-x.

[102] Madonna. Papa Don't Preach. Elliot, B. *True Blue*. Sire Records, Warner Bros. 1986 Compact Disc. Available from iTunes and other online retailers keyword: Papa Don't Preach

[103] Shakespeare, W. *As You Like It*. Act II, Scene VII. 1623. Ebook. Project Gutenberg. Available for download at: http://www.gutenberg.org keyword: As You Like It

[104] *Duets*. Dir. Bruce Paltrow. Hollywood Pictures, et al. 2000. Film. 18-24 minutes. Available from Amazon.com and other online retailers

[105] Ibid., 77-79 minutes

[106] *Mind the Gap*. Dir. Eric Schaeffer. Five Minutes Before the Miracle, et al. 2004. Film. 70-73 minutes. Available from Amazon.com and other online retailers

[107] *A.I. Artificial Intelligence*. Dir. Stephen Spielberg. Warner Bros, et al. 2001. Film. 6-7 minutes. Available to stream on YouTube.com and from Amazon.com and other online retailers

[108] Ibid., 90-93 minutes

[109] Harlow, H, F. *Learning to Love*. 1978. Jason Aronson Inc. ISBN: 978-0876681596

[110] *Lion*. Dir. Garth Davis. The Weinstein Company, et al. 2016. Film 108-110 minutes. Available to stream on YouTube.com and from Amazon.com and other online retailers

[111] *Duets*., 92-97 minutes

[112] *Precious*. Dir. Lee Daniels. Lionsgate, et al. 2009. Film. 93-103 minutes. Available to stream on YouTube.com and from Amazon.com and other online retailers

[113] *We Need to Talk About Kevin.* Dir. Lynne Ramsay. BBC Films. 2011. Film. 103-107 minutes. Available to stream on YouTube.com and from Amazon.com and other online retailers

[114] *Hannah and Her Sisters.*

[115] *Flowers in the Attic.* Dir. Jeffrey Bloom. Fries Entertainment, et al. 1978. Film. 19-26 minutes. Available to stream on YouTube.com and from Amazon.com and other online retailers

[116] *War Horse.* Dir. Stephen Spielberg. DreamWorks, et al. 2011. Film. 42-45 minutes. Available to stream on YouTube.com and from Amazon.com and other online retailers

[117] The *scala amoris* is described by Diotima in Plato's *Symposium.* c385BC. Translation: Jowett, B. Plato's speech. Project Gutenberg. Available for download at: http://www.gutenberg.org keyword: Symposium; *Love and the Ascent to the Beautiful* is also described here: Reeve, C. D. C., "Plato on Friendship and Eros", *The Stanford Encyclopedia of Philosophy* (Summer 2016 Edition), Edward N. Zalta (ed.), URL = <https://plato.stanford.edu/archives/sum2016/entries/plato-friendship/>

[118] Kraut, Richard, "Aristotle's Ethics", *The Stanford Encyclopedia of Philosophy* (Summer 2014 Edition), Edward N. Zalta (ed.), URL = <http://plato.stanford.edu/archives/sum2014/entries/aristotle-ethics/>

[119] Ricky Martin. She's All I Ever Had. Noriega, G. Secada, J. Rosa, D. *Ricky Martin.* Columbia. 1999. Compact Disc. Available from iTunes and other online retailers keyword: She's All I Ever Had

[120] *When Harry Met Sally.* Dir Rob Reiner. Castle Rock Entertainment, et al. 1989. 11-13 minutes. Available from Amazon.com and other online retailers

[121] Ibid., 70-76 minutes

[122] *Friends with Benefits.* Dir. Will Gluck. Screen Gems, et al. 2011. Film. 26-30 minutes. Available to stream on YouTube.com and from Amazon.com and other online retailers

[123] Luther Vandross. If I didn't know better. Vandross, L. Lewis, E. Vertelney *Dance With My Father.* J Records. 2003. Compact Disc. Available from iTunes and other online retailers keyword: If I didn't know better

[124] *Something Borrowed.* Dir. Luke Greenfield. Alcon Entertainment, et al.

2001. Film. 18-23 minutes. Available from Amazon.com and other online retailers

[125] Ibid., 91-94 minutes

[126] *The Soloist*. Dir. Joe Wright. DeeamWorks, et al. 2009. Film. Available to stream on YouTube.com and from Amazon.com and other online retailers

[127] Ibid., 93-97 minutes

[128] Queen. You're My Best Friend. Deacon, J.. *A Night at the Opera*. EMI, Electra. 1975 Compact Disc. Available from iTunes and other online retailers keyword: You're My Best Friend

[129] *The Defiant Ones*. Dir Stanley Kramer. Curtleigh Productions, et al. 1958. Film. 10–12 minutes. Available from Amazon.com and other online retailers

[130] Ibid., 29-36 minutes

[131] Yalom, I. D. *Love's Executioner – And Other Tales of Psychology*. 2012. Basic Books. ISBN: 978-0-465-02011-9

[132] The *scala amoris* is described by Diotima in Plato's *Symposium*. c385BC. Translation: Jowett, B. Plato's speech. Project Gutenberg. Available for download at: http://www.gutenberg.org keyword: Symposium; *Love and the Ascent to the Beautiful* is also described here: Reeve, C. D. C., "Plato on Friendship and Eros", *The Stanford Encyclopedia of Philosophy* (Summer 2016 Edition), Edward N. Zalta (ed.), URL = <https://plato.stanford.edu/archives/sum2016/entries/plato-friendship/>

[133] Plato, through his many works uses the idea of forms, and specifically deals with them in his dialogue *Parmenides* which he considers are unchangeable, eternal, intelligible, divine, incorporeal ideas of being. My application of Platonic forms herein is that of *one over many*, whereby a set of *objects*, in this case real people, are reducible to their phenomenological and abstract quintessential attributes that are true for all objects within a given set. For example, all leaves *are* leaves by sharing quintessential attributes that put them in the set of leaves, even though each is distinctly unique by means of additional attributes beyond the quintessential. This approach *is* simplistic, granted. It neglects some of the underlying issues that surround the use of forms as paradigms, instead concentrating on the single intersecting area of a given Venn diagram, as a class, containing all

and only shared phenomenological and abstract attributes that determine sameness within the class. Detail of the underlying properties of Platonic forms can be found at the www.washington.edu website site: http://faculty.washington.edu/smcohen/320/index.html. (Lecture Notes / The "One Over Many" Argument). Direct link: http://faculty.washington.edu/smcohen/320/1ovrmany.htm. A copy of Plato's *Parmenides* c380BC can be downloaded from http://www.gutenberg.org. keyword Parmenides

[134] Pink Floyd. Fearless. Gilmour, D. Waters, R. *Meddle*. Capitol. 1971. Compact Disc. Available from iTunes and other online retailers keyword: Fearless

[135] The Holy See. (Publication date *unknown*) Catechism of the Catholic Church, Part Three, Life in Christ, Section One, Man's Vocation Life in the Spirit, Chapter One, The Dignity of the Human Person, Article 7 The Virtues. (Charity 1829). Retrieved from: http://www.vatican.va/archive/ccc_css/archive/catechism/p3s1c1a7.htm

[136] Bicentennial Man. Dir. Chris Columbus. 1492 Pictures, et al. 1999. Film. Available from Amazon.com and other online retailers

[137] This quote (L'amour est une étoffe tissée par la nature et brodée par l'imagination) is widely attributed to the French writer, historian and philosopher Voltaire (1694 – 1778). Direct reference to this quote in published works of Voltaire, however, is not available

[138] *For the Love of the Game*. Dir. Sam Raimi. Universal Pictures, et al. 1999. Film. 83-85 minutes. Available to stream on YouTube.com and from Amazon.com and other online retailers

[139] *van Gogh: Painted with Words*. Dir. Andrew Hutton. British Broadcasting Corporation (BBC), et al. 2010. Documentary Film. 0 – 1 minute. Available from Amazon.com and other online retailers

[140] Vincent van Gogh: Letter to Theo van Gogh 2 April 1882. Retrieved from: http://vangoghletters.org. available at: http://vangoghletters.org/vg/letters/let334/letter.html

[141] *van Gogh: Painted with Words*., 18-21 minutes

[142] *New Testament*. King James. Mark 12:30. Available from https://www.gutenberg.org. Keyword: Bible; Deuteronomy 4:29. Available from https://www.gutenberg.org. Keyword: Bible

143 *van Gogh: Painted with Words.*, 25-27 minutes

144 *Educating Rita.* Dir. Lewis Gilbert. Acorn Pictures, et al. 1973. Film. 52-54 minutes. Available from Amazon.com and other online retailers

145 Ibid., 89-91 minutes

146 Noonan, Peggy (January 28, 1986). "*Address to the Nation on the Explosion of the Space Shuttle Challenger*". University of Texas. Retrieved December 27, 2009. The video of this speech is available at: < https://en.wikipedia.org/wiki/Speeches_and_debates_of_Ronald_Reagan#cite_note-15>

147 *Babette's Feast.* Dir. Gabriel Axel. Panorama Film A/S, et al. 1987. Film. Available to stream on YouTube.com and from Amazon.com and other online retailers

148 Ibid., 86-89 minutes

149 Ibid., 97-100 minutes

150 Casablanca. Dir. Michael Curtiz. Warner Bros et al. 1942. Film. Available to stream on YouTube.com and from Amazon.com and other online retailers

151 Von Goethe, J.W., *The Sorrows of Young Werther.* Translator: Boylan, R.D., 2009. Entry: August 28th. EBook. Project Gutenberg. Available for download at: http://www.gutenberg.org keyword: The Sorrows of Young Werther (or Die Leiden des jungen Werther. English). Also available in standard book from Amazon.com: ISBN: 0679643087

152 Ibid., Entry, post-December 20th

153 *Psycho.* Dir. Alfred Hitchcock. Shamley Productions, et al. 1960. Film. Available to stream on YouTube.com and from Amazon.com and other online retailers

154 *Billy Elliot.* Dir Stephen Daldry. StudioCanal, et al. 2000. Film. 85-88 minutes. Available to stream on YouTube.com and from Amazon.com and other online retailers

155 Plato. *Parmenides.* c380BC. Translation: Jowett, B. Project Gutenberg. Available for download at: http://www.gutenberg.org keyword: *Parmenides.* You can also read more on forms at: Rickless, Samuel, "Plato's Parmenides", The Stanford Encyclopedia of Philosophy (Spring 2016 Edition), Edward N. Zalta (ed.), URL =

<https://plato.stanford.edu/archives/spr2016/entries/plato-parmenides/>

[156] *The Purple Rose of Cairo.* Woody Allen. Orion Pictures, et al. 1985. Film. Available from Amazon.com and other online retailers

[157] Ibid., 51-55 minutes

[158] Sartre, J. *Being and Nothingness. The Principle Text of Modern Existentialism.* 1943. First Washington Square Press. pp. 86-95 ISBN: 0-671-04082-0

[159] Christina Perri. Human. *Head or Heart.*

[160] *Black Swan.* Dir. Darren Aronofsky. Fox Searchlight Pictures, et al. 2010 Film. Available from Amazon.com and other online retailers

[161] *What Dreams May Come.* Vincent Ward. Polygram Filmed Entertainment, et al. 1998. Film. Available from YouTube.com and HTTP://www.amazon.com keyword: What Dreams May Come

[162] *New Testament. King James. Revelation 21:11-25*: 21:11 Having the glory of God: and her light was like unto a stone most precious, even like a jasper stone, clear as crystal; / 21:12 And had a wall great and high, and had twelve gates, and at the gates twelve angels, and names written thereon, which are the names of the twelve tribes of the children of Israel: / 21:13 On the east three gates; on the north three gates; on the south three gates; and on the west three gates. / 21:14 And the wall of the city had twelve foundations, and in them the names of the twelve apostles of the Lamb. / 21:15 And he that talked with me had a golden reed to measure the city, and the gates thereof, and the wall thereof. / 21:16 And the city lieth foursquare, and the length is as large as the breadth: and he measured the city with the reed, twelve thousand furlongs. The length and the breadth and the height of it are equal. / 21:17 And he measured the wall thereof, an hundred and forty and four cubits, according to the measure of a man, that is, of the angel. / 21:18 And the building of the wall of it was of jasper: and the city was pure gold, like unto clear glass. / 21:19 And the foundations of the wall of the city were garnished with all manner of precious stones. The first foundation was jasper; the second, sapphire; the third, a chalcedony; the fourth, an emerald; / 21:20 The fifth, sardonyx; the sixth, sardius; the seventh, chrysolyte; the eighth, beryl; the ninth, a topaz; the tenth, a chrysoprasus; the eleventh, a jacinth; the twelfth, an amethyst. / 21:21 And the twelve gates were twelve pearls: every several gate was of one pearl: and the street of the city was pure gold, as it were transparent glass. / 21:22 And I saw no temple therein: for the Lord God

Almighty and the Lamb are the temple of it. / 21:23 And the city had no need of the sun, neither of the moon, to shine in it: for the glory of God did lighten it, and the Lamb is the light thereof. / 21:24 And the nations of them which are saved shall walk in the light of it: and the kings of the earth do bring their glory and honour into it. / 21:25 And the gates of it shall not be shut at all by day: for there shall be no night there. Available from https://www.gutenberg.org. Keyword: Bible

[163] *New Testament*. King James. Luke 23:42-3. Available from https://www.gutenberg.org. Keyword: Bible

[164] *Citizen Kane*. Dir. Orson Wells. RKO Radio Pictures, Mercury Productions. 1941 Film. Available from Amazon.com and other online retailers

[165] Hilton, J. *Lost Horizon*. Original publication 1933. Harper Perennial Reissue . ISBN 0062113720

[166] Martin Luther King Jr. *Where Do We Go from Here: Chaos or Community?.1968. Beacon Press. p. 67*. ISBN: 0807000671

[167] Walt Whitman. Song of the Universe. *Leaves of Grass: A Textual Variorum of the Printed Poems, 1855-1891 (3-Volume Set) (The collected writings of Walt Whitman) 1st Edition*. Volume III. 1980. New York University Press. pp.679-682 ISBN: 0-8147-1014-x-Vol. I; 0-8147-1015-8-Vol. II; 0-8147-1016-6-Vol. III; 0-8147-1024-7 set.

[168] Plato. *Symposium*. c385BC. Translation: Jowett, B Socrates' speech. Project Gutenberg. Available for download at: http://www.gutenberg.org keyword: Symposium

[169] *New Testament*. King James. John 4:7-21. Available from https://www.gutenberg.org. Keyword: Bible

[170] The Holy See. (Publication date *unknown*) *Catechism of the Catholic Church, Part Three, Life in Christ, Section One, Man's Vocation Life in the Spirit, Chapter One, The Dignity of the Human Person, Article 7 The Virtues*. (Hope 1817-1821). Retrieved from: http://www.vatican.va/archive/ccc_css/archive/catechism/p3s1c1a7.htm

[171] Plato *Symposium* eBook 150.2 / 198 Paragraph 3.6. 'This, my dear Socrates,' said the stranger of Mantineia, 'is that life above all others which man should live, in the contemplation of beauty absolute....'. Project Gutenberg. Available for download at: http://www.gutenberg.org

keyword: Symposium

[172] The *scala amoris* is described by Diotima in Plato's *Symposium*. c385BC. Translation: Jowett, B. Socrates' speech. Project Gutenberg. Available for download at: http://www.gutenberg.org keyword: Symposium; *Love and the Ascent to the Beautiful* is also described here: Reeve, C. D. C., "Plato on Friendship and Eros", *The Stanford Encyclopedia of Philosophy* (Summer 2016 Edition), Edward N. Zalta (ed.), URL = <https://plato.stanford.edu/archives/sum2016/entries/plato-friendship/>

[173] Ibid., *Symposium*. Socrates' speech.

[174] The Holy See. (Publication date *unknown*) *Catechism of the Catholic Church, Part Three, Life in Christ, Section One, Man's Vocation Life in the Spirit, Chapter One, The Dignity of the Human Person, Article 7 The Virtues*. (Charity 1829). Retrieved from: http://www.vatican.va/archive/ccc_css/archive/catechism/p3s1c1a7.htm

[175] Ibid., (Hope 1817)

[176] *Old Testament*. King James. Genesis 3:1-23: Available from https://www.gutenberg.org. Keyword: Bible

[177] Gilson, E. *The Mystical Theology of Saint Bernard*. 1940. Cistercian Publications. pp.151-152. ISBN: 0-8790-7960-6

[178] Kraut, R. "Aristotle's Ethics", *The Stanford Encyclopedia of Philosophy* (Summer 2017 Edition), Edward N. Zalta (ed.), URL = <https://plato.stanford.edu/archives/sum2017/entries/aristotle-ethics/>

[179] *New Testament*. King James. The Second Epistle of Paul the Apostle to the Thessalonians 1:3: Available from https://www.gutenberg.org. Keyword: Bible

[180] Freud, S. *Group Psychology and the Analysis of the Ego* - Section V. Para 9 Available from https://www.gutenberg.org. Keyword: Group Psychology and the Analysis of the Ego

[181] The Holy See. (Publication date *unknown*) *Catechism of the Catholic Church, Part Three, Life in Christ, Section One, Man's Vocation Life in the Spirit, Chapter One, The Dignity of the Human Person, Article 7 The Virtues*. (Charity 1817). Retrieved from:

http://www.vatican.va/archive/ccc_css/archive/catechism/p3s1c1a7.htm

[182] Sabine Baring-Gould. 1834-1924. *Onward, Christian Soldiers.* Hymn

[183] Asbridge, T. *The Crusades – The Authoritative History of the War for the Holy Land.* 2010. Harper Collins. ISBN: 0-7432-6860-1

[184] *Jonestown The Life and Death of Peoples Temple.* Dir. Stanley Nelson. Firelight Media Inc (PBS). 2006. Film Documentary. Available from Amazon.com and other online retailers

[185] *New Testament.* King James. John I 5:7 For there are three that bear record in heaven, the Father, the Word, and the Holy Ghost: and these three are one. Available from https://www.gutenberg.org. Keyword: Bible

[186] Ibid., Mathew 22.37-38. Available from https://www.gutenberg.org. Keyword: Bible

[187] *Old Testament.* King James. Job. Available from https://www.gutenberg.org. Keyword: Bible

[188] *Merchant of Venice.* Dir. Michael Radford. Movision, et al. 2004. Film. Available from Amazon.com and other online retailers

[189] *New Testament.* King James. John I 4:19. Available from https://www.gutenberg.org. Keyword: Bible

[190] Ibid., John I 4:11-12. Available from https://www.gutenberg.org. Keyword: Bible

[191] Frankie Goes to Hollywood. The Power of Love. Johnson, H. Gill, p. O'Toole, M. Nash, B. *Welcome to the Pleasuredome.* EMI Music Publishing. 1984. Compact Disc. Available from iTunes and other online retailers keyword: The Power of Love

[192] *New Testament.* King James. John 14:22-23. Available from https://www.gutenberg.org. Keyword: Bible

[193] *Old Testament.* King James. Genesis 1:31. Available from https://www.gutenberg.org. Keyword: Bible

[194] *New Testament.* King James. John I 4:19. Available from https://www.gutenberg.org. Keyword: Bible

[195] Ibid.

[196] The extract below from *Hosea* is the description of God's bestowal of love as a covenant, with ownership of the beloved through a groom marrying a bride, with those who take up the Word of God and love Him as their Lord (within the context of Christianity in this instance). *Old Testament.* King James. Hosea 24:1: *And in that day will I make a covenant for them with the beasts of the field and with the fowls of heaven, and with the creeping things of the ground: and I will break the bow and the sword and the battle out of the earth, and will make them to lie down safely.* **And I will betroth thee unto me for ever; yea, I will betroth thee unto me in righteousness, and in judgment, and in lovingkindness, and in mercies. I will even betroth thee unto me in faithfulness:** *and thou shalt know the LORD. And it shall come to pass in that day, I will hear, saith the LORD, I will hear the heavens, and they shall hear the earth; And the earth shall hear the corn, and the wine, and the oil; and they shall hear Jezreel. And I will sow her unto me in the earth; and I will have mercy upon her that had not obtained mercy; and I will say to them which were not my people,* **Thou art my people***; and they shall say, Thou art my God. Then said the LORD unto me, Go yet, love a woman beloved of her friend, yet an adulteress, according to the love of the LORD toward the children of Israel, who look to other gods, and love flagons of wine. So I bought her to me for fifteen pieces of silver, and for an homer of barley, and an half homer of barley: And I said unto her, Thou shalt abide for me many days; thou shalt not play the harlot, and thou shalt not be for another man: so will I also be for thee.* Available from https://www.gutenberg.org. Keyword: Bible

[197] Singer, I., *The Nature of Love, 1 Plato and Luther*. 2009, The MIT Press. pp.160. ISBN: 978-0-262-51272-5.

[198] Tylor, E.B. *Primitive culture: researches into the development of mythology, philosophy, religion, art, and custom.* New York: Gordon Press. 1974. ISBN: 978-0-87968-091-6

[199] *New Testament.* King James. Ephesians 6:5-8. Available from https://www.gutenberg.org. Keyword: Bible

[200] *New Testament.* King James. Mark 12:30. Available from https://www.gutenberg.org. Keyword: Bible

[201] *Pulp Fiction.* Dir. Quentin Tarantino. Miramax, et al. 1994. 146-150 minutes. Film. Available to stream on YouTube.com and from Amazon.com and other online retailers

[202] *Old Testament.* King James. Genesis 22:1-24 Available from https://www.gutenberg.org. Keyword: Bible

NOTES AND REFERENCES

www.ingramcontent.com/pod-product-compliance
Lightning Source LLC
Chambersburg PA
CBHW021945290426
44108CB00012B/964